DUE DATE

Icarus World Issues Series

Coca-Cola Culture
Icons of Pop

Series Editors, Roger Rosen and Patra McSharry Sevastiades

THE ROSEN PUBLISHING GROUP, INC.
NEW YORK

Published in 1993 by The Rosen Publishing Group, Inc.
29 E. 21st Street, New York, NY 10010

First Edition

Library of Congress Cataloging-in-Publication Data

Coca-Cola culture : icons of pop/[edited by] Roger Rosen and Patra McSharry Sevastiades..
    p. cm. — (Icarus world issues series)
    Includes bibliographical references and index
    ISBN 0-8239-1593-X.—ISBN 0-8239-1594-8
    1. Popular culture—United States. 2. Popular culture—American influences. I. Rosen, Roger. II.Sevastiades, Patra McSharry. III. Series.
E169. 12. C545   1993
306.4'0973--dc20   93-24147
                                           CIP
                                           AC

Manufactured in the United States of America

Contents

Introduction

I had just completed an arduous journey to an isolated monastery on Mount Athos in northern Greece. My head was full of illuminated manuscripts, Byzantine frescoes, and choral music from stops along the way. Ushered into a courtyard to meet the abbot, I was told that English was not one of his languages. He entered with the last light of evening, wearing a long black cassock. The heavy gold crucifix around his neck blazed with a chance streak of refracted sunlight. He looked into my eyes and nodded with the understanding of realized consciousness. He opened his mouth. I strained to understand. "Kojak," he said. "Kojak?" I replied. "Kojak," said he with approval. And not another word for the rest of my visit.

No one could have provided me with a better icon of pop.

*   *   *

America bashers love to talk about that museum of the future in which next to the Elgin marbles, the friezes from Nineveh, and the bronze doors of the Benin are displayed a crumpled Mars Bar wrapper and a crushed can of Coke. Those cynics will tell you that when it comes to cultural imperialism the spoils quite clearly go to the country with the biggest market share, and the U.S.A. is very obviously winning. So culture follows gold. This is not news. When Britannia ruled the waves cricket came to be played in Islamabad while Matthew Arnold was set to be memorized in Nairobi. Any empire-building worthy of the name brings with it the home team's vision: Leaving home without it is simply bad for business. Going native lets the side down.

In the late twentieth century, fashion pundits applaud the sagacity of those merchandisers who have discovered the advantages of marketing not just products, but lifestyles. And yet, looking at the archaeological finds at sites throughout the Mediterranean or along the Silk Route, the Turquoise Trail, or any other trading center you care to mention, you cannot help but feel that every piece of pottery, pair of earrings, adze, or ax sold far from home was imbued in its day with a provenance that conjured up whole worlds. Today a billboard in a city square conveys the message. In a bygone era the goods might have emerged from a bit of gossamer within a silk purse inside a carpet bag between a camel's humps. In whatever time zone we travel, someone is tampering with something. Some aspect of reality has been packaged.

The twelfth volume of the *Icarus World Issues Series*, Coca-Cola Culture: Icons of Pop, is about taste, power, politics, propaganda, rock music, mice without genitals, the movies, carbonated beverages, dream machines, blue jeans, and Marlboro cigarettes. Our authors have looked at the ways in which Americana has influenced both the world and our thoughts about ourselves. Reading the numerous submissions for this issue, some of our staff have come to the conclusion that you're not what you eat but what you export. We'll be interested to know what you think. In that museum of the future, will it be a Mars Bar, a Stinger missile, Mickey, or the Bill of Rights that finds its way into that vitrine that has been reserved for us? After all, there might not be too much room. Someone might just have to choose.

Roger Rosen, Editor

FREEZE-FRAME POLAND 1979

POLISH COWBOYS AND MARLBORO MEN

CARL ROLLYSON

Carl Rollyson was born in Miami, Florida. He received his PhD in English from the University of Toronto and teaches at Baruch College of the City of New York.

Professor Rollyson is the author of several biographies, including *Picasso, The Lives of Norman Mailer, Lillian Hellman,* and *Marilyn Monroe.* He has received several awards, among them a grant from the National Endowment for the Humanities, a Fulbright Fellowship, grants from the American Philosophical Society and from the American Council of Learned Societies, and Faculty Research Awards from the City University of New York. His biographical essays have also appeared in numerous journals and collections of biography.

Professor Rollyson is currently working on a biography of Rebecca West. He lives in Brooklyn with his wife, Lisa Paddock, and their 16-year-old daughter, Amelia.

I try to imagine the emerging new Poland: a gray skyline iridescent with golden arches, ambiance of neon, glittering signs lighting up a consumer culture: Coke bottles and Marlboro boxes packaging life in ways that Americans take for granted in an open marketplace that now extends to more than half the world. When I arrived in Communist Poland in 1979 to begin my year as a Fulbright Lecturer at the University of Gdansk, the world was still divided into the halves dictated by a Cold War mentality. And although that division was never quite so simple (as terms like the "Third World" and the "nonaligned powers" suggested), I encountered overwhelming numbers of Poles who behaved as though there were only two blocs, led by the Soviet Union and the United States.

One of the first things I noticed in Poland was the lack of packaging. When you shopped at supermarkets, popularly known as SAMS, you brought your own bag to carry away your purchases. If you bought eggs, they would be loaded into a paper bag and would probably break in the inevitable jostling of a crowded bus. Except for a few foreign items—such as orange juice imported from Greece—brand names were rare. Polish supermarkets did not put their brand name on items, did not associate the identity of a product with their name, and did not stimulate shoppers' appetites with attractive colors, shapes, and designs. Their commodities had no fizz; your mouth didn't water before you opened them; nothing was new and improved. Instead, there were aisles and aisles of dull cardboard boxes filled with macaroni and cookies and detergent. I once told a Polish friend that I had finally discovered the difference between a SAM and a Super-SAM. "Oh?" he said, surprised because no one so far as he knew saw any difference. "More macaroni," was my triumphant reply.

3

Did it really matter that Poland was not a land of brand names? Isn't advertising really a joke serving no useful purpose except profits? I observed that it mattered to all kinds of Poles in the streets where I shopped, in the parks and restaurants, the bistros and hotels. There I saw Poles wearing American clothing—especially jeans. An American was welcomed not only as a source of dollars, which bought the finer things in life, but as someone who was free to indulge in the trademarks of mass consumer society, who could effortlessly proclaim simply by attire that he or she was a part of the healthy, aggressive, appetitive culture of America.

What Poles were exposed to through their media was highly selective. American movies were shown on television and in theaters, though often films that had failed in the United States, like "Avalanche," would be the sorry pick of the week. A Pole could not buy an American newspaper in a shop or at a kiosk, and the news on television and in the press was heavily censored. Yet many Poles had managed to visit the United States and had worked there earning precious dollars, and many had American relatives. As a result, Poles were up-to-date, but more important, Poles were moved by American symbols and stories.

In 1989, three of the most popular programs on Polish television were "Rich Man, Poor Man," "Dallas," and "Kojak." Though masses of Poles resisted Communist propaganda, common sense told them that capitalism made for rich people and poor people and that the gap between the two was dramatic. But like many American melodramas, "Rich Man, Poor Man" is about the American dream: Anyone potentially can make it big. That many people do not is beside the point to a dreamer. Poles were dreamers and romantics in a system that had leveled their dreams and had provided them with substandard living conditions, of which they were contemptuous because they knew they could do better. It always seemed to me that Poles were Americans in embryo, so passionate was their attachment to American products and personalities.

"Dallas" was enormously popular because it put a face on American acquisitiveness and made it into a family drama. J. R. was a villain, but a villain in a competitive society. He was corrupt, but he had rivals, he could be brought down, he could be shot! Compared to the color-less leaders and faded packaging of Polish society, "Dallas" expressed an exuberance and a world divided between haves and have-nots. Poles knew it was simplistic, but it also was a refreshing alternative to their sense of politi-cal reality. A Pole had to have a friend in government or at work who could grease the way past the bureaucratic, monopolistic practices of the state. In "Dallas," individuals and families could build their own empires, and the state was largely an irrelevance.

That "Dallas" was set in the Southwest was an important factor, for Poles loved cowboys for all the reasons Americans do. Cowboys are independent, rugged, and stoic. Cowboys smoke Marlboros, the most popular American brand of ciga-rettes in the country. There was even a factory in Poland pro-ducing them, and some Poles said the cigarettes were stronger than the American variety. Everyone smoked, and my Polish friends laughed when I once showed up at a party with a package of Polish cigarettes that fell apart. For Poles, Marlboros evoked not merely the image of the lone cowboy on a horse, entirely responsible for his own des-tiny—the tall-in-the-saddle cliché—they paradoxically defined the group. Under Communism, Poles were dissi-dents by nature, radical individualists with a great romantic tradition. To be a Polish cowboy—as my friend Max called himself—was to be the ultimate form of dissident. His name, in fact, was Waclav, and he spoke only broken English, but he smoked Marlboros like a champ.

No single product or icon summed up the Polish fascina-tion with American popular culture quite the way

5

Marlboro did. Coke and Pepsi, for example, had divided the country between them, with Coke reigning in the North and Pepsi in the South. Not everyone smoked Marlboros, of course, and they were favored by men more than women, but they represented quintessential Americanness to Poles, to taxi drivers and university professors, the people likeliest to initiate a conversation with me and offer me—yes—a Marlboro.

The appearance of a product should not be discounted, the sheen of possession that put a gloss on a Pole's style. American packaging wasn't flimsy. When you finished a pack of Marlboros, it made the good, solid crisp noise of something just a little resistant to the hand that crumples it, the satisfying sound that succeeds human consumption. I'm convinced that Poles missed those sounds in their own mass-produced "goods"—a misnomer if ever there was one. Their pathetic cartons and containers simply didn't have the rewarding scrunch of a well-packaged consumer item. It is the very repetitiveness of such simple, palpable pleasures that drives a consumer economy, and the Poles craved more of it. I began to grasp the appeal of American popular culture to Polish eyes when I returned to the States for the Christmas holidays. After several months of immersion in the centralized command economy of Poland, where every meat shop had a sign identical to every other, every paper store the same display as the next, and so on, landing in New York was dazzling. The lights of Manhattan seen from the air were electrifying. The airport bathroom was a revelation: the fixtures so solid, precisely the opposite of the rickety, white plastic apparatus of Polish plumbing.

Returning to Poland I realized that packaging is more than surface; it broadcasts in an extravagant way the inner works of the product. What's inside seems magical because of what covers it. It isn't just soap when it comes in a beautiful aquamarine package; it is Zest! No wonder the unwrapped bar becomes the occasion for breaking out in a shower song. This is foolish, but Americans love it, and the Poles were starved for it. The icons of packaging make washing up not a chore, but a happy celebration Americans all participate in, and we all know it. We all know that millions of bars are sold. For Poles such American items mean participation in a world community of consumerism, a largely American community because everyone knew that the pursuit of happiness was written into our Constitution—not simply our Declaration of Independence, but our character. A Pole admired that American sense of freedom, and to remind Poles—as I sometimes did—that Americans too suffered hardships was to remind them of something that they already knew but that made no impression; not when every American, even the poorest of the poor, could clutch a Marlboro pack.

Such icons packed power because anyone could buy them, wear them, taste them, devour them, and expect an endlessly renewable supply. The only price was the price on the package. You did not have to be a Party member, a black marketer, a privileged official. For only a few dollars you could possess what Coke called "the real thing."

By contrast, the Polish economy seemed to have been founded on the principle of maldistribution and shortages. When I arrived in Gdansk in the fall of 1979, my local supermarket had a stack of orange juice cans from Greece that almost reached the ceiling. Each week the pyramid lost a bit of height until it vanished altogether. The supply was never replenished. Only one kind of hard cheese was available. Then one day I saw cheddar; the next week it was gone. Bananas and oranges appeared fitfully, causing long lines of harried shoppers to shout instructions to the clerks: "Sell no more than half a kilo. Save some for us. This is a long line!" I took a trip south to Lublin and returned to Gdansk with several cans of corn. "Where did

7

you get this stuff?" my astonished Polish friends wondered. They could not remember ever seeing canned corn in their markets.

Poles understood that America and American popular culture was more complex than the neat, perfect, gleaming veneer of its merchandise, but American logos and labels, wrappers and bags, symbolized the material and the immaterial, the body and the spirit of a creative, dynamic culture. It seemed awesome to them. I remember being asked several times: "How can you possibly choose between so many different versions of the same product? Don't you get confused?" If suddenly thrust into such a bazaar of alternatives, many of them thought they would be confused. They wanted more, but could one really cope with, say, a choice that went beyond Coke or Pepsi? What kind of epistemological breakthrough would it have taken for Poles to accustom themselves to the concept of the "Uncola"?

Of course, it takes almost no time at all for people to adjust to a consumer economy, and it is revealing that when Communism finally died, the Polish choice was to move overnight—or at least as rapidly as possible—to an open marketplace. In other words, those Cold War fears in 1979 were largely theoretical, a habit of mind ingrained in deprived consumers who for the moment could not conceive a higher good than their Marlboro packs.

Marlboro is a tough, strong smoke—so the ads say. For Poles, I'd call it a Kojak smoke. If America's packaging stood the test of a good crunch, had sharp edges and wore well, its human icons, like Kojak, seemed just as tough. Kojak was leathery and durable, an urban cowboy in the clothes of a cop. A cowboy because he was his own man, tightly put together, who did not need a Stetson because that shaved head suggested that he had shorn himself down to the essentials. He might be employed by the state, but like a true American hero he was his own man, doing things his way, on the case like Kojak—the name itself a kind of brand with a good crunch to it.

Kojak—it sounds vaguely Eastern European, a shortened American variant of a Polish name like the ones Poles have come up with here—as my grandfather did, shortening his name from Sokolnicki to Sokolik. Kojak is short and sharp, like a two-syllable expletive that has a hammer-blow propulsiveness to it. It is easy for a Pole to pronounce and to identify with.

Were there Polish Kojaks? Yes, in the sense that there were Polish cowboys within the system bucking the system. Take my friend Max, for example, the self-proclaimed Polish cowboy. He was studying for his Ph.D. in philosophy; he was also teaching at the university and was required to teach the mandatory course in Marxism which he scorned but did not protest. He expressed his dissent in other ways. In fact, it seemed to me his life was organized around the idea of making himself into a "character" in precisely the way Kojak is a character. But Max was fighting the crimes perpetrated by the state—above all, its attempt to censor and to prevent distribution of knowledge. In his apartment he had an enormous archive of the ephemera of dissent: the notes and flyers and announcements of meetings, film showings, guest speakers, graffiti of all kinds—anything he could tear off a wall or bulletin board before the authorities confiscated it, this record of a counterculture. I remember his telling me one day about a film that I had to see. It was being shown that afternoon.

Tired after a day of teaching and wanting to go home, I demurred. "Maybe some other time," I said. "You don't understand," Max shook his head, "if you don't see it now, you won't see it again." What was most important, most truthful, was what you could catch on the fly—hence the origin of the term "Flying University," an institution organized by Poles who attempted to teach the truth about subjects suppressed or diluted in the government-controlled universities.

Max carried on his dissident work with admirable swagger. He didn't have a ten-gallon hat and chaps, but he did like to mimic the words of cowboy-individualists like Kojak, and he enjoyed grilling me about American slang. He was a sophisticated man; he knew Kojak was a myth. He also knew that he was creating his own myth in Gdansk, the birthplace of Solidarity, whose own logo became part of a worldwide phenomenon that eventually brought down Soviet-style Communism.

The Soviets and their satellites scorned the superficial commodity-driven Western economies with their Coke-bottle symbols. The West was sweet and syrupy and soft, indulging in a false sense of individualism catered to by the sham of advertising. Although Poland's Communist authorities did not want their people corrupted by Capitalist icons, the government nevertheless cut its deals with the West, especially America, allowing in small amounts of popular culture as a sop to its people and as a source of hard currency.

Even though Poland's Communist government had its own symbols, they literally paled beside the vibrant American ones, whose power was quantitative and qualitative. There was so much of it and it all held together so well; it was all of a piece. In Poland, on the other hand, the bright red emblems of Communism shone in a wasteland, a crumbling infrastructure that often meant blackouts and brownouts for several hours every day, lack of hot water, lack of essential medicines, and pollution that not only made the water unsafe to drink, but in certain regions, such as Krakow, increased the incidence of respiratory disease and caused the steady disintegration of the ancient city's extraordinary cathedrals and museums. The disparity between the government symbols and the state of society was so great that it became the source of much black humor.

By contrast, American culture never lost its fizz. Every bottle of American beer or cola would effervesce. Only one brand of Polish beer was worth drinking; the rest tasted watered and flat. And this idea, that an individual's taste would be satisfied every time and in the same way by a product, was immensely appealing. About the only Polish product that reliable was vodka, but indulging in it left you senseless. It also reminded Poles of the paucity of their choices.

When I think back on it now, those Poles who expressed their fear that a multitude of choices would confuse them were voicing their amazement at the American cornucopia. They were tremendously excited by the daunting prospect of having so much at hand, but liked it all the more because it was daunting and appeared to be a mountain worth climbing. Few Poles, for example, could afford cars. The Communist solution: the installment plan with a catch. You could buy a car in installments, all right, but you did not get the car until you paid all the installments! And that proved to be a six- or seven-year ordeal. Poles waited in line for virtually everything and often heard the words *"Nie ma,"* "No more, we don't have it," said in disgruntled, hostile tones by bored clerks.

The frame is unfrozen now, and Poles are rapidly capitalizing, turning over the means of production to the private sector, establishing an American-style banking system, and many small businesses. They are entrepreneurs. Of course, they always were entrepreneurs, always on the lookout for the latest in American goods, which were, ipso facto, good. Do they expand in comfort under the golden arches, or are they confused? Of one thing I'm sure: As they sort through the chaos of incredible social change, Marlboro men and Polish cowboys still ride the range.

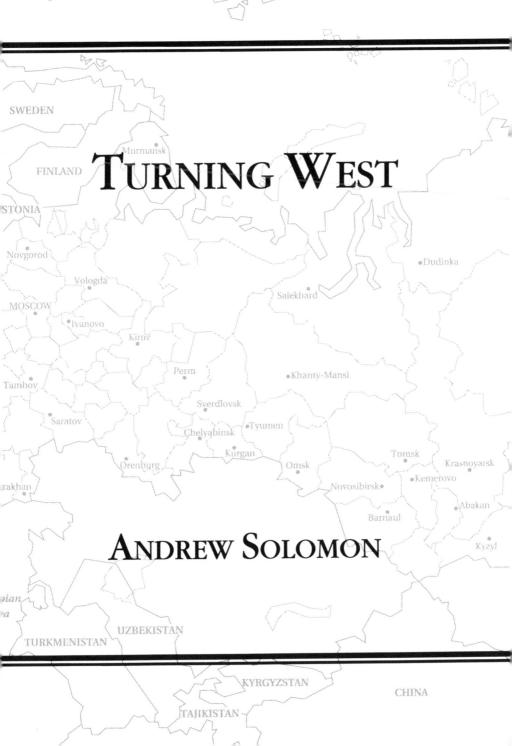

TURNING WEST

ANDREW SOLOMON

© 1992 Christopher Makos

Andrew Solomon received degrees with honors in English at Yale University and at Jesus College, Cambridge University, England. He has received numerous awards, including the Mrs. Claude Beddington Prize, the Quiller-Couch Prize, the J. W. Elsworth Prize, and the Yale Conservation Project Fellowship.

Mr. Solomon is a contributing editor of the *New York Times Magazine*, for which he writes on topics of cultural politics. He has also held editorial positions at *HG* magazine, Hearst in London, and the Metropolitan Museum of Art. His work has appeared in newspapers, magazines, and books around the world, among them *The TLS*, *Dagens Nyheter Stockholm*, and *Moscow News*. He is the author of *The Irony Tower: Soviet Artists in a Time of Glasnost*.

Mr. Solomon divides his time between New York and London. His new book, *A Stone Boat*, will be published in England in 1994.

It is late at night, and I am deep in conversation with Andrey Khlobystin, a Petersburg conceptualist, who this evening sports trendy 1970s Soviet green nylon bell-bottoms and a pair of platform shoes. "The situation of the new generation in Russia," he explains, "is like the situation of the first generation after Copernicus. We have had to come to terms with the idea that the world in which we live, which we had supposed to be the center of everything, is in fact only a remote and rather uninteresting corner of a vast universe; and that what we do we do only for ourselves, since that vast universe could continue virtually unchanged if our world disappeared."

In the wake of this revelation, Russians are undergoing a profound transformation in which they strangely mix anger at their reduced station with wild delight at their new freedoms. In the old Soviet system, Russians were told that they were the envy of the rest of the world; and though the intelligentsia knew the society was rotten at its core, many ordinary Russians were persuaded that the military power and geographic scale of the Soviet Union made it the greatest country in the world. Russians were given little access to knowledge of life elsewhere. No Western television came through. No Western magazines were sold. Western art and music and literature were kept at bay. Russians were told that their country was superior, but they had little occasion to understand to what it was superior.

With the advent of *glasnost* (literally, "openness"), Western influences began to infiltrate the country. Many Russians, traumatized by the dawning revelation that their country had not been the most glorious of all, went into a shocked depression. But among others, especially the sophisticates who had never bought into the myth of

Soviet supremacy, there was an ardor for things Western that was often almost manic. Whatever had been forbidden or unavailable in the Soviet period became fascinating. Though some Western ideas were considered and reinterpreted, most were simply taken over whole hog. Westerners, eager to exploit the naive enthusiasms of Russians, foisted the worst of Western popular culture on the unsuspecting people, and the result is that the society is now glutted with the cultural detritus of our own. So dazzled are the Russians by the glamour of the West that they often fail to distinguish between the better things Americans have to offer and the worse ones. It is fascinating to see Russian responses to Western popular culture and Western technology, to see both how much exuberance the Russians can bring to what strikes Americans as old hat, and how readily they can lose themselves in the lowest sort of Western junk. It is fascinating but terrible to see how much Americans have contributed to the cultural chaos that now reigns in Russia.

It is the weekend of Orthodox Easter, and I am in St. Petersburg, at the home of Viktor Frolov. Under Soviet rule, the night before Easter was a big party night in Russia. The state organized activities, such as the showing of otherwise forbidden Western films, to distract people from the religious festival. That tradition lives on. Tonight, we are to go to a Russian rave—Kristall II, at the ice-skating rink.

Raves originated in Great Britain in the 1980s and later spread to the United States. These underground parties, protected by secret telephone numbers and locations, were all-night affairs for an elite drug subculture. One had to know both the right people and the right argot to be invited. In Russia, raves have taken on a different character.

At about two o'clock on Easter morning, we pile into a few old cars and a taxi and drive off to the skating rink, where several thousand people have already gathered.

Frolov, a twenty-six-year-old smooth operator with all the right connections in all the right places, goes first. He says something to the man at the door; we are admitted free. Inside, the sound system is turned up so high that the vast building shakes; there is a mix of live music performed by a visiting Dutch band and recorded Western and Russian music. There is a laser show and a bar. On half of the rink, people are skating to the music. The other half has been boarded over to make a dance floor. Friends push one another from the dance floor onto the ice, where people slide back and forth in street shoes, sometimes falling over each other. A few minor fights break out on the ice. In the grandstands, people smoke hashish, and sometimes pass out.

The dancers possess seemingly inexhaustible energy. The floor is alive with bodies all night, but the feeling is strikingly asexual. People dance and skate in groups of three or four, or they pair up with friends of their own gender. It does not seem that anyone is picking anyone else up. There is a lot of conversation. In some ways, this is like an all-night cocktail party.

The music is relentless, technomusic. "There should be a better mix," says a connoisseur. "Some house, some rap. A whole night of techno"—he shrugs—"but the real moment for raves is past." It is generally agreed that raves are now passé, but everyone has nonetheless come this evening. This is the norm in the new Russia. "The fashion is over," explains painter Georgiy Guryanov, "but there's nothing else to do."

Our group leaves at 6:30. The sun is coming up. "Where to now?" someone asks, and we drift off to the apartment of other friends, where we eat whole jars of jam (I am almost as hungry as I am exhausted) and the leftover end of an elderly sausage, and watch music videos on TV. We get home at about eight o'clock on Easter morning.

*   *   *

The Russian rave scene began in Moscow in December 1991, four months after the failed coup that led to the downfall of Mikhail S. Gorbachev and brought Boris N. Yeltsin to the highest levels of power. The original Russian rave, the First Gagarin Party, was organized by Yevgeniy Birman and Alexey Haas. It was held at the Cosmos Pavilion at VDNKh, Stalin's park of industrial exhibitions, and attracted more than 4,000 people. I spoke with Birman and Haas, both in their late twenties, the geniuses behind the entire Russian rave scene; they argued after the First Gagarin Party (named after national hero Yuriy Gagarin, the cosmonaut), and have since worked separately. "The First Gagarin was so amazing because everyone was so hungry for it, after all those dreary Soviet years," explains Birman, who has a loose, expansive manner and a round boyish face. "It was our gift to Russia."

The First Gagarin Party was an unparalleled flirtation with finesse. Lasers bounced off the rich interior of the Cosmos Pavilion, the ultimate Stalinist temple to the achievements of the socialist state. Western DJs served up the latest music. The crowd was incredibly sophisticated; you would not have guessed that Russia held 4,000 such people. "I proved to myself that these people did exist in Moscow," Haas told me, "the people who could make a party like this a success. I drove around in my car in the weeks before the party, and when I saw people of the right sort, I gave them invitations and told them to bring their friends. I gave complimentary invitations to a thousand friends. On the day of the party we ran ads on TV. They were in English, to select the audience."

Haas's subsequent raves have been enormously success-ful. "I want to work with the energy of the people," he explains. "When I first went to the West, I traveled to Stockholm, and I visited a club with technological effects I'd never even dreamed of. But the people there were dancing like fish. Then I went to a club in New York that just had good music in a black room and young people who were totally alive. I understood that that was what I needed."

These parties are really the product of Russian perceptions of a Western idea, and they are successful because of the way they change. Though the music and the lasers and the concept are very Western, the quality of the events is somehow very Russian. Here, the Russian longing for Western standards has pushed the Russians beyond their usual scope. But the ice in Petersburg, the conviviality of the events, the mix of Russian warmth and an affected notion of "coolness" results in something that could not exist elsewhere, something that is, in its way, quite wonderful.

At a birthday party at which the soundtrack to "The Cook, The Thief, His Wife, and Her Lover" is playing relentlessly, a man with long hair, in his early twenties, is introduced to me as Kirill Preobrazhenskiy, "a true Moscow cyberpunk." He and I chat for a few minutes. "Excuse me," I say, "but do you really define yourself as a cyberpunk?"

Kirill is visibly embarrassed. "Well, not exactly. But I'm into interactive television, virtual reality, computer bulletin boards, all that stuff. I've been trying to set up a video link to the West, but I can't because all our satellites are controlled by people who hate technology, Communist leftovers from the old Soviet TV. And I can't afford to bribe them at the current level."

"Tell me about computer bulletin boards," I say.

"It's incredible," Kirill assures me. "It's a big obsession. People everywhere, especially across Siberia, get into these enormous discussions. Everyone with a computer: people working at companies, usually, using the computers themselves, at night."

"What do you talk about?" I ask.

The question evidently strikes Kirill as curious. "Nothing

much," he replies. "It's not important what we say. Those in Siberia tell me that their lives are very boring and very repetitive and very cold and very lonely. So what? We all know that. It's the technology that's interesting."

In Russia, technological knowledge is still rare, and it is cherished by those who have it. Even as someone who has just learned to ski may take pleasure in the act of skiing itself, without thought of the landscape he is seeing, the incline of the slope, or the quality of the piste, so Russians are fascinated by their newfound capacity to use technology, without regard to actual ends to which that technology might lead them. So what is useful but not necessarily pleasurable in the West becomes not so much useful as joyous in Russia.

I have dinner with M. C. Pavlov, who was previously the drummer of rock band Zvukimu. His new band, M. D. and C. Pavlov, has been rising in popularity. Pavlov is intentionally keeping out of the serious pop scene. He has avoided involvement with the Russian mafia and does not have his videos shown regularly on TV. But he does make videos, and his albums are available; his concerts are increasingly popular. He is the only true rap artist in the country.

The role of contemporary music has been completely transformed in Russia in the last two years. In the '70s and early '80s, rock music was the voice of the underground; lyrics described the possibility of a better life-style to people trapped within the constraints of the Soviet system. Rock music was heroic. The performers, closely tied to the intelligentsia, were more immediately attuned to day-to-day political developments than were the gray-suited members of the Politburo. As Pavlov observed, "Heroic Russian rock was for listening to like a political speech, but it wasn't for dancing."

There were also many pop musicians in this period, but

they represented official culture and were part of the Soviet establishment. Though their music was often on the radio, few listeners paid much attention; indeed, they were generally seen as interchangeable. While an almost cultish following attached themselves to the leading rock musicians, pop fans were happy with whatever star the government-run radio was championing.

"Soviet Russian culture," Pavlov says, "was completely nonrhythmic. If you look at people at ordinary Russian concerts, you'll see that they try to clap along with the music, because they've seen videos that show Western audiences doing that. But they're never on the beat. We just wanted to bring some fun into this country. So what we do, it's some rap and some house and some R&B and some jazz."

Pavlov represents an amalgamated music unique to Russia. Based on ideas from Western contemporary music, it is altogether unlike anything actually heard in the West. "We're not black. Nor red. We're white," concedes Pavlov. "We're not from the 'hood. We know that. It was a big fashion here, we did it too, to try to integrate blacks into our performances. But we decided that that was a little fake. We're trying to be ourselves, more."

"There were too many styles, and they came all at once," the artist Dmitriy Prigov explains. "Ideas never arrive in our country one by one; in Russia, we receive ideas that have developed independently of one another in bundles, and we always suffer under the impression that they have more in common than they have to distinguish them, and so we create chimeras of our own."

The director of music programming for Russian National Television, Artyom Troitsky, was one of the heroes of the Russian Rock movement; he chronicled and wrote about every new stage and development. In the 1970s, when he was in his twenties, he explained, fighting the KGB was a big adventure. "The situation was incredibly simple. They

21

were black and we were white. For us, the simplest thing was to be moral." But in Russian society of the 1990s, chaos and confusion reign. "For young people today," Troitsky says, "the simplest thing is to live well, because they don't understand what everything else is all about. Materialism is where it's at."

This may explain the remarkable shallowness of the new Russian pop. With simple and repetitive tunes and cotton candy lyrics, the lion's share of this music relies on inept renderings of Western themes. I watch TV videos endlessly. Many of them are expensively produced, but the performers look ridiculous. Pornographic references of any kind were forbidden in the Soviet era; now you can view a blond woman with thickly applied makeup singing to her lost sailor that, whatever happens, he is the only train for her, and she will always be his train station. Music of the Soviet era bore no relation to violence. Now, captivated by the brutality of American pop music, Russians produce videos of people shooting each other, and the gangster-heroes of the videos are beginning to show up with alarming frequency in real life. It's not simply that the political heroism is gone: It's that a kind of antiheroism has taken its place.

Music is not the only thing to be found on TV. There are also absurd game shows that combine every principle of Western materialism: On one of them, families run after paper money that is being blown around by jets of hot air. It's the worst kind of greedy materialism, founded on the principle of every man for himself. "That's the message of Western pop culture," a singer I know tells me ruefully. "Capitalism. Take for yourself, and then keep taking, and don't give away anything."

The last two years have also seen the introduction of the soap opera to Russian society. Producers for Russian national television bought the cheapest one they could find, a glorious fiesta of cliché, produced in Mexico in the early '70s, called "The Rich Also Cry." The program features actress Veronica Castro as Marianna: Her image is plastered everywhere in Russia these days. The show became so popular that some Russian factories were forced to close from three to four o'clock in the afternoon, when the show was on, because the workers were simply walking away from the machines to go home and watch. In a survey conducted earlier this year, the three names most consistently recognized by Russians were, in order: Boris N. Yeltsin; Mikhail S. Gorbachev; and Veronica Castro.

At one level, this is hilarious. Sophisticated Muscovites joke about it all, as do visitors from the West. But the real effect of the mindless exporting of Western junk culture is dire indeed.

The attention that the West pays to the former Soviet Union is perceived at the moment as a matter of protecting its own self-interest. America has made financial investments, but has not been generous with its culture. During the Gulf War, America brought into play a great deal of the rhetoric of democracy: America defended Kuwait, it was said, because Americans in their idealism could not tolerate the triumph of totalitarianism. In the republics of the former Soviet Union, however, America invokes no such rhetoric. America does have a role to play in Russia. The Yeltsin government is fragile, and it is in the best interests of the West—for economic and military reasons, and for the sake of global stability—to bolster that government. The most effective way to do so is to speak with passion and conviction about democracy itself, to present persuasively the vision so well articulated by America's founding fathers, which ostensibly continues to play a defining role in American life. Democracy is not a matter of the capitalistic self-interest that American popular culture celebrates. Democracy is an ideological system with both material and immaterial benefits.

It has been a strongly held American belief that free and powerful artistic expression flourishes in a democracy, that it is in a society such as America's that artists can speak out most eloquently. But America's complete lack of interest in exporting any of its "high culture" and American carelessness in regulating the profiteering export of "low culture" has left most people in the former Soviet Union laboring under the impression that the fruit of democracy is not rich and various artistic expression, but second-rate soap operas, glitzy rock videos, and thriller/horror fiction. Though all the nations of the West share blame for inadequate representations of democracy in the former Soviet Union, this is an area in which America has been particularly remiss. The German and the Scandinavian and the French governments have all made a passing though wholly inadequate effort to exhibit the best of their cultural output; the American government has made no effort at all. Instead, individual organizations promote their own agendas in a nation that lacks an understanding of the American context. On every bus in Moscow last winter, there were enormous posters advertising Billy Graham; one news broadcast, put together by credulous Russians and generally unchallenged, described him as "apparently the most important thinker in America."

Of course, the most enlightened people in the former Soviet Union do understand what it means to strive for democracy; and the least enlightened people in the former Soviet Union don't care. It would, however, be a mistake to overestimate the number of sophisticates who have a full grasp of the Western system; it is only too easy, if you live in the West, to imagine that the ties between free trade and a free society are obvious. They are not obvious, and they can remain obscure even to people of immense intellectual accomplishment, especially if those people have not traveled. American exports of popular culture serve to further the confusion.

Last December, I found myself on the steppe in Kazakhstan, sitting in a yurt, drinking fermented mare's milk with a group of yak herders. "The Westerners who ordinarily come here," said the eldest one, "are businessmen and diplomats; and I have enough experience of the world to know that it is not the work of businessmen and diplomats to tell the truth. But you are a writer, and it is your work to tell the truth. If our society comes closer to yours, that will be of great benefit to these diplomats and businessmen. But for us—will we be happier?" He gestured around the yurt. "Our lives are not so bad. We're not so unhappy. We eat well enough, and have sheep for the slaughter. You have traveled a great deal. What do other societies have, what does your society have, that we don't have? I have seen these American television programs with the big buildings and the people shooting each other. I don't think that looks better in any way than our lives here."

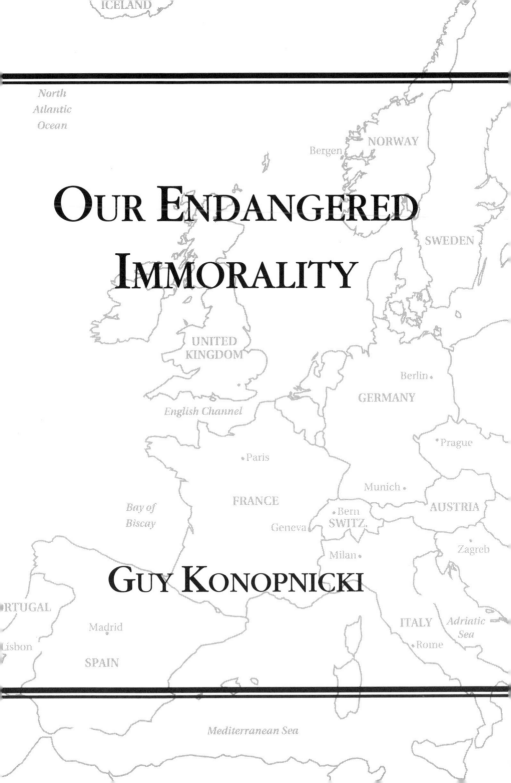

OUR ENDANGERED

IMMORALITY

GUY KONOPNICKI

Guy Konopnicki was born in Paris. He is a novelist, essayist, and screenwriter. Mr. Konopnicki studied literature and sociology at the University of Nanterre and at the Sorbonne, where he also participated in the student movement of 1968.

Mr. Konopnicki is a regular contributor to Radio France and to the review *La Règle du Jeu*. He has published three novels and a dozen essays. Two of his new books, a novel and a thriller, will be published in 1994.

In addition, Mr. Konopnicki, a member of the Ecology Party, was elected to the Regional Council of Ile de France in 1992.

Mr. Konopnicki lives in Paris.

The woman who steps forward to testify in the Paris Law Court seems confused. She looks around for the chair facing the audience, the Bible upon which she must swear, she expects a duel between lawyers in three-piece suits. She doesn't know, she no longer knows that the witness stands before the witness stand, that the defendant is seated between two police officers in the accused box, and that the French Republic does not mix God and the Bible with human justice. She has seen dozens of trials on TV, American TV series trials. Her country's own judicial system seems strange to her.

Even more tragic is the case of a young man in a police station who is screaming and protesting: He wants to make a telephone call. The police answer him with laughter. There will be no "quarter," no "telephone call" for him. He will not have his rights read to him as in the movies. When a child in the Parisian suburbs, he had been raised on American TV series and had seen dozens of arrests, with police officers reading accused criminals their rights and the possibility of telephoning a lawyer. Police custody French style surprises him.

These are just two everyday anecdotes. They demonstrate that reality is truly less familiar than television. Sooner or later, one must discover not America, but the Atlantic ocean. The American judicial mythology has become universal. It is true that French law owes the belated introduction of several Anglo-Saxon habeas corpus statutes to this universality. But along with the American mythology that is beamed abroad, a myth inevitably emerges: that of a judicial system based on an unquestionable morality.

In France, the protectors of the law—I am referring to the judges—are really no different from the accused. But

29

in the past few years, they have begun attacking fortresses and confronting politicians. It is true that French politicians are nothing but great criminals who are upheld by an unquestioned legitimacy, that of universal suffrage. Until recently, these politicians believed themselves to be the sole preservers of the Republic. Judges were (and remain) nothing but civil servants. However, events in America have transformed French judges. We now find them defending a very unusual cause against politicians—morality.

Although across the ocean it seems self-evident, I daresay that morality is a totally new requirement in France, a country where Jesuits triumphed over Jansenists*, where the Terror of 1793 proved itself powerless to make virtue triumphant. This is because France has always kept itself free by means of a libertine and redeeming corruption such as that of the Regent Philippe on the heels of the strict moral order imposed by Louis XIV, and the unbridled luxury of the Directory** after Robespierre.*** More recently, the Third Republic (1870-1940), which was the longest-lived French regime, survived both scandals and corruption, neither of which prevented it from establishing a considerable empire or producing extraordinary results. For this is the "corrupt" republic that covered France with schools, built democratic and egalitarian institutions, and regulated the development of capitalism with social legislation. The politicians of today, whom judges tirelessly pursue, are angels in comparison with one-time premiers Jules Ferry and Edouard Herriot.

---

*Jansenism arose among some French Catholics in the 17th century in response to the perceived laxity of the Jesuits. It demanded morally rigorous behavior.
**Directory—the counterrevolutionary body of five directors that ruled France from 1795 to 1799.
***Maximilien Robespierre (1758-1794)—French lawyer and a key leader in the French Revolution (1789).

I will even go as far as to claim that the most perverse of French fantasies about America concerns justice. Motivated by an idealized vision of American justice, accompanied by a certain Watergate syndrome, French judges and journalists dream of having their own Watergate and of resembling the law enforcers of American television series. In my opinion, this is even more dangerous than the showy presence of Eurodisney at the gates of Paris. Eurodisney is merely harmless little Mickey bringing strange versions of the original Charles Perrault fairy tales back to France. Our problem does not lie therein! I am more worried by the puritanism, by the good intentions, by the prudish morality that is threatening the decadent legacy of Rabelais and Laclos. A century ago, in France, the President of the Republic received his mistress at the Elysée Palace. Senators and representatives more frequently went to the bordello than to church. A politician spotted with a top model became a national hero the following day.

Alas! A moral wind is blowing from the Far West. A politically correct wind that comes along to revive our straitlaced Catholicism. And it is being sent to us from the great Protestant country, formerly a refuge for our persecuted Huguenots*! Morality, health, diet! Stuffed to the gills with American television programs, French television is nibbling away at lay epicureanism. It has introduced God as a celebrity, accompanied by images of sweet little children saying their prayers every night. American TV programs are succeeding where the Vichy regime failed: They are in the process of re-evangelizing France!

The liberties that the French so cherish were conceived and established by republicans with big bellies who preached progress after feasting on banquets washed down with plenty of wine. Most of them lived long lives despite gout or syphilis. They even took a certain pride in

---

*Hugenot—a French Protestant in the 16th or 17th century.

these diseases, which were contracted at banquets or at orgies. Their Republic was personified by an attentive, lavishly caring Marianne, and when she appeared on French coins sowing liberty, she exposed a very nice derriere and shapely calves for the whole world to see.

But Madame Bovary finally gave way to the preachers of the Western. French presidential candidates now invent childhoods worthy of Abraham Lincoln. Young representatives want to be Mr. Smith in the Senate.

France's immersion in American culture will, in the end, have given the French exactly the opposite of what its opponents of the past feared. To think that they were predicting the depravation of French morals by the invasion of the sex-symbols of American cinema. In reality France is bombarded with good intentions, overwhelmed by sugar-coated morality and puritan justice.

It is worth defending French immorality from this sugary evangelization which the crusaders of the satellites are forcing upon us.

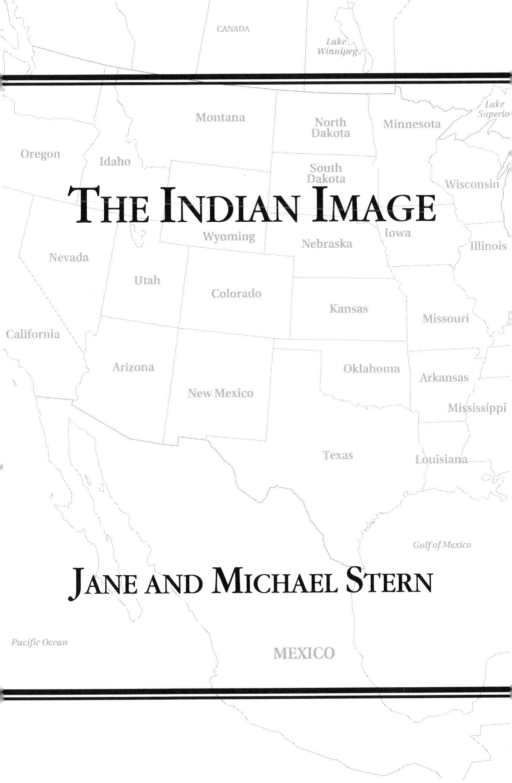

THE INDIAN IMAGE

JANE AND MICHAEL STERN

Jane Stern was born in New York City and Michael Stern in Chicago. Ms. Stern received a bachelor's degree from the Pratt Institute in Brooklyn and a Master of Fine Arts degree from Yale University. Mr. Stern received a bachelor's degree from the University of Michigan and later a Master of Fine Arts degree from Columbia University. For twenty years they have traveled the United States and written about American culture.

The Sterns are the coauthors of eighteen books, including *Elvis World, Sixties People,* and *Jane and Michael Stern's Encyclopedia of Pop Culture.* They are reporters-at-large for *The New Yorker.* Their work has appeared in *Redbook, GQ, Spy,* and the *New York Times,* among other publications. They have appeared on "Good Morning, America," "The David Letterman Show," and "60 Minutes." They are frequent guests on "National Public Radio."

The Sterns live in Connecticut. The following selection is an excerpt from their forthcoming book *Way Out West,* to be published in November by HarperCollins.

Should you ask me, whence these stories?
Whence the legends and traditions,
With the odors of the forest,
With the dew and damp of meadows,
With the curling smoke of wigwams,
With the rushing of great rivers,
With their frequent repetitions,
And their wild reverberations,
As of thunder in the mountains?

—from "The Song of Hiawatha" by
Henry Wadsworth Longfellow

In 1907, the American Indian became the best-known Western advertising image prior to the Marlboro cowboy. That was the year the Santa Fe Railway issued the first of its annual calendars, featuring paintings of Native Americans engaged in tribal activities or simply looking august and exotic. Hundreds of thousands of these calendars, meant to be enchanting invitations to visit the Southwest, were sent free throughout the land each year for more than three quarters of a century. The railroad had tickets to sell; and the Indians on the calendars (as well as in advertising) proved to be a compelling lure. "The Santa Fe Indian," writes T. C. McLuhan in *Dream Tracks*, her enlightening book about the impact of the railroad on Southwest Indian life, "possessed an aura of glamour. An intangibility. An ineffable essence. . . . Simplicity. Freedom. Nobility." Even before that first calendar, the Indian image had become a powerful symbol of the West, and it has remained a symbol ever since—so powerful that it has obscured the reality of Indian life.

The true story of America's native peoples, and of what happened to them as the West was won and their lands

35

were lost, has been called this nation's great unfinished business. It is a story that is grand and colorful, gilded with lofty ideals, stained by wave upon wave of unspeakable tragedy, and almost always tinged by fear and fascination—and misunderstanding—on the part of white people. "Why do you call us Indians?" a tribesman asked Pilgrim Missionary John Eliot in 1646. As Robert F. Berkhofer, Jr. points out in *The White Man's Indian*, there were some two thousand cultures in North America when white people arrived; each saw itself as separate and distinct. But the newcomers lumped them all together and misnamed them, simply because Columbus thought he had landed somewhere near India.

(The proper name for indigenous Americans is still very much an issue. Some tribal spokespeople prefer "Native American," which is technically correct. For the most part, though, Native Americans we have encountered in our travels still frequently use the term "Indian," at least when talking to outsiders. Among themselves they are unlikely to use either "Indian" or "Native American"; instead, "Navajo," "Choctaw," "Cherokee," etc. are the words that really express who they are. Some tribes are battling even these labels. A faction of Navajo want to shed the word *Navajo*, which was derived from the Spanish term *Apaches de Navajó* ["*Navajó*" was the Spanish name for what is now northern New Mexico and Arizona], and return to what they used to call themselves—Diné, meaning simply "people." The former Papagos—also a Spanish name, meaning "bean people"—who live in the Sonoran desert south of Phoenix, Arizona, have already officially reclaimed the more traditional name Tohono O'odham, meaning desert people.)

One reason for this tribal interest in reclaiming original names is that the rest of America has always felt free to appropriate the names, as well as the likenesses, of indigenous peoples for products of all kinds: Red Man chewing tobacco, Crazy Horse beer, Navajo Van

Lines, Chevrolet Apache trucks, and Jeep Cherokee station wagons. High school, college, and professional sports teams traditionally adopt names such as "Indians," "Braves," and "Chiefs" for their connotation of never-say-die ferocity. In the last few years, the Atlanta Braves fans' rallying gesture—the tomahawk chop—has become a sore point among many Native Americans and their sympathizers, who see it as a disrespectful cliché. (Actually, a freehand chop was originally devised in the early 1980s at Florida State to cheer on the University's Seminoles; it became a Braves' thing in 1991 only after a foam-bedding salesman named Paul Braddy began marketing foam tomahawks.)

For Indians, it has not necessarily been a wonderful thing that their image—however exalted, ferocious, or magical—has veiled their existence as human beings. One original obstacle to perceiving the native peoples of this continent as equal beings was that the United States was founded on a firm belief in natural law at a time when nature and all things close to it were thought to hold the key to truth and virtue. "Nature itself had become holy," write William H. Goetzmann and William N. Goetzmann in *The West of the Imagination.* "Primitive people [were equated with] nature and nature's laws, thus making them, in their grand simplicity, the people closest to God." So while the natives of America represented a problem to be reckoned with—they had to be evicted from their homelands for westward settlement to proceed—they also took on a role in white people's eyes as nature's truest surrogates. The complexities and refinement of their ancient cultures notwithstanding, Indians became the country's own race of "noble savages." They were considered primitive and therefore close to earth and wise in the ways of cosmic law.

James Fennimore Cooper's Leatherstocking tales, *The Last of the Mohicans* in particular, helped crystallize this sentimental image of a heroic race doomed by the onslaught of civilization. George Catlin, originally of Philadelphia, put it on canvas in lyric paintings that depicted the Indians of the West (and of the East) as a glorious breed of people, enveloped in nature's dignity; in his words: "their long arms in orisons of praise to the Great Spirit in the sun, for the freedom and happiness of their existence." Writing about the red man he painted, he described him as being "in the innocent simplicity of nature, in the full enjoyment of the luxuries which God has bestowed upon him...happier than kings and princes can be, with his pipe and little ones about him." He described his subjects as "Lords of the forest" and "Nature's proudest, noblest men," and the West they inhabited as "the great and almost boundless garden spot of the earth."

In 1840, some fifty years before Buffalo Bill Cody toured Europe with his Wild West Show, Catlin opened an "Indian Gallery" in London (and subsequently in Paris). Here he displayed his paintings of buffalo hunts and tribal ceremonies. He also employed his nephew to put on paint and do a war dance for patrons; he gave archery demonstrations and delivered lectures on the use of the tomahawk and the peace pipe. His presentations always focused on the lamentable fact that native peoples were being uprooted by westward movement across the U.S. To Catlin, the Indian was a vanishing idol, a victim of the march of civilization. He wrote, "From the towering cliffs of the Rocky Mountains, the luckless savage will turn back his swollen eyes on the illimitable hunting grounds from which he has fled; and there contemplate, like Caius Marius on the ruins of Carthage, their splendid desolation."

Catlin was so disturbed by the awful effects of settlement on Indians and their lands that as early as 1842 he wishfully imagined the West being transformed into a kind of huge nature preserve, where Indians, like an endangered species, would be protected. It would become "a *magnificent park*, where the world could see for ages to come the native Indian in his classic attire, galloping his wild horse,

39

with sinewy bow, and shield and lance, amid the fleeting herds of elk and buffaloes...A *nation's Park*, containing man and beast, in all the wild and freshness of their nature's beauty."

The enduring influence of Henry Wadsworth Longfellow's epic poem "The Song of Hiawatha," published in 1855, was the result in great measure of its setting in the past, on the verge of the coming of the white man. Its Indians were not a roadblock in the way of manifest destiny; they were a simple, happy people living in harmony with the earth—and gladly welcoming the black-robed missionary who comes to convert them to Christianity at the end. Written in drum-beat meter like a legend chanted around a campfire, the poem's idyllic descriptions of the ways of the Ojibway and Dacotah cast a nostalgic spell so powerful that even as a policy of bloody extirpation was being waged against intransigent Natives, thousands of school children learned to recite the poem—to honor America's first people. Young white students donned dyed feather headdresses and mock buckskin and delivered their verse complete with an elaborate system of hand signals to indicate a wigwam, a rising moon, and baby Hiawatha being rocked in his linden cradle "safely bound with reindeer sinews." The most oft-repeated part of the heroic tale was from the section titled "Hiawatha's Childhood":

> By the shores of Gitche Gumee,
> By the shining Big-Sea-Water,
> Stood the wigwam of Nokomis,
> Daughter of the Moon, Nokomis.
> Dark behind it rose the forest,
> Rose the black and gloomy pine trees,
> Rose the firs with cones upon them;
> Bright before it beat the water,
> Beat the clear and sunny water,
> Beat the shining Big-Sea-Water.

By the time Buffalo Bill Cody began to mythologize the frontier in his Wild West shows in 1883, it was impossible to envision the West remaining wild any longer. The frontier was on the verge of being "closed." The West had been won; Indian resistance had been broken; and with rare exception, the surviving Indians had surrendered. "Some of my best friends were Indians," Cody once boasted, speaking in the past tense; and out of friendship—as well as showmanship—he made them part of his spectacle. Along with longhorn cattle, buffalo, coyotes, and cowboys, Indians became featured players in the exhilarating pageant of the frontier that originally defined the pop-culture West.

Most of the Indians employed in the Wild West Show were Dakota Sioux, and thanks in part to their featured role in Buffalo Bill's pageant, they became *the* symbolic Indians of North America. It was the Sioux who camped in circles of white tepees (their word was *tipi*); they painted their ponies for war; they smoked a peace pipe; and they wore spectacular eagle-feather headdresses, fringed buckskin shirts, and beaded moccasins. To many people unaware of the diversity of Native American cultures, they became the total and complete image of the American Indian.

And of course under the direction of Buffalo Bill, who knew that audiences would not spend money to see peaceable natives sitting together in equanimity, they did their best to yelp and cavort and behave as wild Indians were supposed to do. They chased after a covered wagon train, ululating and wielding their tomahawks; and in a grand melodramatic finale, they massed as an army of feathered savages and recreated "Custer's Last Charge"(the word *stand* was then considered too defeatist), including battle with the US cavalry on horseback, hand-to-hand knife and fist fights, and a chilling climactic moment when a Sioux brave reached down to take the scalp of General George Armstrong Custer. Imagine

41

the awe and horror the audiences felt when, immediately after this blood-curdling mayhem, Hunkpapa Sioux chief Sitting Bull—the very man who had directed the massacre of Custer's troops less than ten years earlier—rode out before them in full-feather regalia. Many in the audience took the opportunity to jeer Sitting Bull as Custer's murderer.

After one season with the Wild West Show, in 1885, Sitting Bull (a US government captive since 1881) was allowed to go to the Standing Rock Sioux reservation in Dakota, and Cody—with whom he had become fast friends—gave him a gray horse from the show. It was a trick horse that had been trained to sit and wave its hooves in the air at the report of a gun. In 1890, at the height of the Ghost Dance frenzy (a belief that spread through many Western reservations that wild—but peaceful—dancing would bring forth an Indian Messiah who would renew the buffalo herds, restore Indians to their lands, and make white men vanish), Major General Nelson Miles ordered the rearrest of Sitting Bull for fomenting the allegedly subversive cult. (It was a trumped-up charge; in fact, Sitting Bull was skeptical of Ghost Dancing.) When police came, more than a hundred Ghost Dancers rallied to protect the venerable chief; in the confusion, shots were fired. At the sound of the guns, Sitting Bull's horse began to perform, sitting on its haunches and waving a hoof in the air as it had learned to do in the Wild West Show: an unsettling coda to the image white men had created for the vanquished chief. The Sioux leader, whom the police later accused of resisting arrest, took a bullet and fell dead. But his horse continued to perform in the midst of the melee, stunning onlookers who thought the horse itself had been seized with the Ghost Dance spirit.

Even before the Ghost Dance cult animated the Plains reservation dwellers and became a catalyst for the final awful massacre at Wounded Knee in the Badlands in 1890, the Indian wars had come to a symbolic close in the Southwest when Apache chief Geronimo surrendered for the last time in 1886 in Skeleton Canyon, on the Arizona–New Mexico border. Geronimo, already notorious as the "Tiger of the Southwest" for his ability to wage guerrilla war and to elude capture, became the most famous Apache in America. After serving time at hard labor in Florida, Geronimo was allowed to appear in Pawnee Bill's Wild West show, billed as "the worst Indian that ever lived." Outfitted in flamboyant eagle-feather headdress, he rode before the crowds in a Locomobile touring car, gunning down a live buffalo from the passenger seat, a performance advertised as "The Last Buffalo Hunt." Never mind that as a Chiricahua Apache of the Southwest mountains, it is likely that Geronimo had never seen a buffalo in his life and had never worn head-feathers: He had become the supreme image of an Indian on the warpath; and that image, in the popular mind, necessarily included a warbonnet as well as a wake of dead buffalo.

Indians soon became a prime tourist attraction in the Southwest. Subdued and no longer an obstacle to settlement, they still carried a whiff of danger about them, providing the traveler with the kind of wild-game park thrill George Catlin had once imagined. Beyond their curiosity value as an only recently defeated enemy, Indians were also valued for their intrinsic interest and for their craft skills. The opening of Hotel El Tovar at the rim of the Grand Canyon in 1904 gave visitors not only a close-up view of nature, but also a view of America's natural people—Indians—making jewelry at Hopi House, a crafts studio built by the Fred Harvey Company just across the way from the hotel. In Albuquerque, Harvey's Alvarado Hotel opened an entire room devoted to the display (and sale) of Native people's pottery, baskets, jewelry, and rugs.

By the 1910s Indians had become a quintessential symbol of the frontier: its glories and its tragedy. Artist James

Earl Fraser had planned his famous 1915 sculpture "End of the Trail" (showing an exhausted brave on an equally exhausted horse) from the time he was a boy in Dakota Territory, when he heard a hunter predict that eventually all the Indians would be driven into the Pacific Ocean. Fraser also put a regal Indian on the Buffalo nickel in 1913, which along with the Indian-head penny (according to legend, modeled after Sarah Longacre, a white engraver's daughter, who posed wearing a warbonnet), literally put the image of the Indian into the hands and pockets of every American. For many years, "End of the Trail" was a common motif in knicknacks—ashtrays, bookends, etc.— meant to inspire sentimental thoughts of vanquished nobility, not necessarily about Native Americans.

The Santa Fe Railway calendar first issued in 1907 was not merely a collection of majestic portraits of Natives. Featuring works by Taos artists who had become enraptured by the land and culture of New Mexico, it showed the Indians' life in the most romantic way possible—their campfire ceremonies, dances, hunting parties; their ancient pueblos; the gorgeous land that was once theirs alone. The writer D. H. Lawrence, one of the literati who had found the Southwest to be a spiritual elixir, wrote in 1924, "The skyscraper will scatter on the winds like thistledown, and the genuine America, the America of New Mexico, will start on its course again." Before that apocalypse, there were plenty of tourists—Easterners as well as Europeans—who were eager to leave the land of skyscrapers and come see the genuine Americans.

In 1926, encouraged by the success of El Tovar and tour buses that took tourists around the rim of the Grand Canyon, the Santa Fe Railway, in conjunction with the Fred Harvey Company, introduced "Indian Detours." Now someone traveling coast to coast by rail could pay extra and stop in Winslow, Albuquerque, or Santa Fe for a guided excursion into Indian country. Groups of

Detourists stepped off the train and boarded elongated Packard Harveycars with eleven upholstered swivel seats and broad Pullman-style windows for two- or three-day tours into Indian country. Each car was driven by a cowboy-mechanic in a ten-gallon hat and riding boots; and each was hosted by a specially trained "courier," a college-educated white woman in an Indian velvet shirt and silver concha belt. According to company literature, the couriers all had supplemented their education with "special training on archaeological and ethnological history." Their job was to make the trip an experience that brought travelers so close to Indians they could touch them:

> Greeting guest upon arrival by train, it is
> thereafter their privilege to fill the
> pleasant dual role of hostesses as well as
> guides. Couriers' friendships with
> representative Indians in many pueblos assure
> their guests of intimate glimpses of Indian
> life not otherwise obtainable.

Detourists stayed in ranches and guest houses and spent their time watching Indian ceremonies, buying crafts, and taking pictures of exotic scenes. Comfortable walking shoes were recommended, for although the Harveycars traveled in areas virtually devoid of roads, in many places tourists were invited to step out and stroll through the magic land. They were promised walks "along the paths of the Indians, worn inches deep in solid rock by moccasined feet" and "buffet lunch served among the pines beneath the Puyé cliff, in the long firelit lounge of a unique rest house constructed of building stones from the prehistoric pueblo above."

In the same year Indian Detour service began, the Santa Fe line introduced its first all-Pullman train, called the Chief, which ran between Chicago and Los Angeles, via Indian country. Ten years later, the Super Chief debuted; each of its

45

Every inch the Chief

Santa Fe

sleepers had a name that evoked Pueblo peoples—*Isleta,*. *Taos, Laguna*—and each was fully fitted with Indian-motif decor. *In his History of the Atchison, Topeka and Santa Fe Railway,* Keith L. Bryant, Jr. writes that the *Navajo* car featured a "turquoise ceiling, goatskin lamp shades, sand paintings encased in glass, and upholstery based on Navajo designs."

Just as movies consummated the transformation of cowboy from hired man to folk hero, they further flattened the Indian image into a familiar stereotype. Hollywood's Indians were mostly based on the whooping Sioux of the Wild West shows, and while silver-screen red men have ranged from tragic innocents to bloodthirsty demons, certain aspects of their roles in movies have been consistent: Indians are always symbolic of something; and they are usually clichés, outfitted in what Ralph and Natasha Friar in *The Only Good Indian* describe as the "instant Indian kit" of buckskin and warbonnet, with tomahawk and bow and arrow. They all live in tepees, pound drums, ride beautiful paint horses, and communicate in an elementary language of grunts and hand signs. They are simple people—simple and happy or simple and wicked, depending on what the plot requires.

In John Ford's "The Iron Horse" (1924) and "Stagecoach" (1939) and thousands of cowboy movies that followed, they are faceless savages on horseback, symbols of the frontier's perils, pursuing white people for no other reason than an insatiable lust for scalps. In sympathetic pictures such as "The Vanishing American" (1925, about a World War I Indian veteran who sees his people brutalized by whites), they represent a noble culture that embodies nature's harmony and is victimized by settlement. It is rare in Westerns that feature Indians to find a Native-American character with any kind of personality that goes beyond these wooden-Indian formulas, regardless of whether that character is supposed to be honorable or brutish.

In the first half-century of the movie business, Indians in most Westerns were seldom personally vilified; they were simply anonymous hordes who had to be killed or subdued so that white men could win the West. There were rare exceptions to this pattern, but scenes of howling savages in war paint became as common a motif in Westerns as the shoot-out and the runaway stagecoach.

Despite the number of rampaging Indians killed in his movies, director John Ford was so appreciated by the Navajo of Monument Valley, whom he regularly hired (at full union wages) to act in his Westerns, that they named him *Natani Nez* (Tall Soldier); and Harry Goulding of Goulding's lodge and trading post (where the film crew stayed on location) once said, "To the Navajos, Mr. Ford is holy, sorta." Late in his career, Ford tried to redress the savage image of his earlier movies in the bitterly apologetic "Cheyenne Autumn" (1964), from Marie Sandoz's novel about the tragic march by Cheyenne in 1878 from Oklahoma to their home on the Yellowstone. Even so, however, the plum "Indian" roles were played by Caucasians with swarthy skin: Riccardo Montalban as Little Wolf, Gilbert Roland as Dull Knife, Sal Mineo as Red Shirt, Victory Jory as Tall Tree.

In the 1950's Hollywood's image of Indians began to change. Starting with Delmer Daves's "Broken Arrow" (1950), about a white man in love with an Apache girl (played by Debra Paget, not an Apache), it became more common to see Indians depicted as innocent victims rather than scalp-hunting fiends. There had always been a number of red men who were trusty sidekicks, such as the Lone Ranger's Tonto. And of course there were plenty of comic characters, such as Chief Thunderthud and Princess Summerfall Winterspring on television's "Howdy Doody." But after "Broken Arrow," such movies as Robert Aldrich's "Apache" (1954) and Douglas Sirk's "Taza, Son of Cochise" (1955) actually purported to deal with the

Indian question as a troubling issue in need of solution; both movies set forth a policy of peaceful coexistence.

Indians were the subject of a great cultural vogue starting in the late 1960s, thanks mostly to hippies, who liked to see themselves as tribal sorts of people. Headbands, moccasins, body paint, and turquoise jewelry were adopted by flower children as symbols of their closeness to North America's original tribes. Wearing beads became "a symbolic rejection of a corrupt society and a return to the communal values of American Indians," announced student rebel Ted Kaptchuk in a 1968 *Eye* magazine fashion story. In *Flashing on the Sixties*, which includes an account of the New Buffalo hippie commune in New Mexico, Lisa Law writes, "The Indians of the Taos Pueblo helped the New Buffaloers by being friends and teachers, and the young Indians in turn gained self-respect when they saw other men with long hair."

In 1971, the Raiders (formerly Paul Revere and the Raiders) hit the top of the *Billboard* chart with "Indian Reservation (The Lament of the Cherokee Reservation Indian)," about the sad fate of Native Americans forced to live on reservations. Originally written by John D. Loudermilk in 1963 and recorded by Don Fardon in England, it became a monster hit in the U.S.—the biggest-selling single in Columbia Records' history to that date. Two years later Cher went native in Bob Mackie beads and buckskin for her "Sonny and Cher Comedy Hour" on television and sent "Half Breed," a socially conscious song, to the top of the record sales charts.

As national shame over the Vietnam War escalated, the cause of Indians became a favorite among many concerned people in the entertainment business, who saw parallels between U.S. government policies toward the indigenous people of the American West and those of Southeast Asia. Starting in 1970 for about half a dozen years, Hollywood produced dozens of diligently pro-

49

Indian, anti-Army pictures. "Soldier Blue" (1970) set the tone; billed as "the most brutal and liberating, the most honest American film ever made," it was about the Army's 1864 Sand Creek slaughter of Indians. According to the director, it was meant to parallel the My Lai incident in Vietnam, and it is shocking in its depiction of senseless bloodshed (mostly by whites against Indians). It featured a plaintive title song written and performed by Cree activist and folk singer Buffy Sainte-Marie; however, the Indians in the movie were mostly anonymous, and all the major roles were played by whites (including Candice Bergen and Peter Strauss). Another 1970 picture, "A Man Called Horse," was scrupulous in its attempt at realism, including dialogue spoken in Lakota Sioux; nevertheless, *The BFI Companion to the Western* quotes the Native American newspaper *Akwesasne Notes* about it: "Same old savage stereotype. White actors playing cigar store Indians." Reportedly, the Sioux who allowed the film to be made on their reservation became "the laughingstock of Indian America."

Chief Dan George, an actor from the Tse-lal-watt tribe of British Columbia, provided audiences with another perspective on Native Americans in the 1970s: He had a sense of humor. First as Old Lodge Skins in the savage history lesson "Little Big Man" (1970, from the novel by Thomas Berger), then as Lone Watie, Clint Eastwood's traveling companion in the resonant epic "The Outlaw Josey Wales" (1976), he provided both films with unexpected tenderness. George's addition of whimsy to the Indian image has been echoed in many films since, perhaps most effectively in "Thunderheart" (1992), about an earnest FBI agent (Val Kilmer) who comes to terms with his mystical Indian heritage while solving a murder. Spiritual as its plot may be, "Thunderheart" is notable for the pranks and fun enjoyed by its Indian supporting cast: Graham Greene as a witty tribal cop, and Chief Ted Thin Elk as a shrewd old Sioux medicine man addicted to television shows who always seems to be hoodwinking Kilmer.

The single best-known Indian image of modern times is probably Cherokee actor Iron Eyes Cody, who posed for an antilittering advertisement in 1972 with a tear falling down his right cheek. The tear was not for the fate of Native Americans but for the plight of the American landscape. His sorrowful face was featured in television public-service advertisements (and subsequent posters) produced for Keep America Beautiful, Inc. The ads show him surveying an American countryside that his people used to respect and keep clean, but now white people smother with tin cans, fast-food wrappers, and other unsightly litter. "Pollution: It's a Crying Shame," the ad copy says. This may be the first time an Indian ever wept on TV or in the movies—stoicism in the face of tragedy has always been part of the Indian image—and it proved to be one of the most striking advertising campaigns of the decade.

Another memorable moment in the evolution of the Indian image occurred in 1973, when Marlon Brando sent Apache actress Sacheen Littlefeather to the podium at the Academy Awards ceremony to *refuse* his best-actor Oscar (for "The Godfather"). Ms. Littlefeather told the Motion Picture Academy that Brando was turning down the award because Indians were so poorly treated in movies. However, Kim Newman's enlightening book *Wild West Movies* points out that in fact during the early 1970s the movie industry was obsessed with redressing wrongs done to Indians, and it did so by exalting and ennobling them in such pictures as "A Man Called Horse," "Little Big Man," and "Billy Jack" (1971), which turned the tables and showed white men as devils. Newman writes, "One would be hard pressed to pick through Westerns made since 1972 and find an unsympathetic, disrespectful portrayal of a Native American. . . . It seems that Hollywood is ashamed of everything the white man has done to the red, except patronizing him."

After a decade in which Indians were little seen in movies, director-star Kevin Costner revivified the noble image in "Dances with Wolves" (1990), which *U.S. News & World Report* declared the catalyst for a new era of "Native American chic." Costner's romantic parable extolled the Lakota Sioux as loving, peaceable, loyal, emotionally expressive, ecologically responsible, and joyous people who find themselves besieged by U.S. soldiers who are nothing but evil scum. As Union officer Dunbar, Costner is so smitten with the Sioux that he changes sides and joins them, even falls in love with one (who happens to be a white woman raised by them, thus allowing the plot to dodge the issue of intermarriage). When they name him Dances with Wolves, he declares that he knows for the first time who he really is. Audiences loved the three-hour fable, and the Motion Picture Academy named it the year's best movie.

Some critics welcomed "Dances with Wolves" because it appeared to be history from the Native American point of view. In a *Ms.* magazine article, Marilou Awiakta wrote, "For the first time, a highly commercial film portrays Native Americans as individuals—intelligent, complex, humorous. *Civilized.*" Nevertheless, the movie had many detractors. In *The New Yorker*, Pauline Kael called it "a kid's daydream of being an Indian." Like so many Westerns of years past, its heroes were pure and virtuous beyond belief; in this case, the good guys wore buckskin and head feathers, and the savages had white skin. Like "The Song of Hiawatha," and so many sentimentalizing Indian fantasies going back centuries, "Dances with Wolves" put red men on a pedestal as symbols of Nature's wisdom, and in that sense once again denied them their humanity.

We recently stumbled across a Western scene that said a

lot about the enduring power of the Indian image in contemporary life. In Window Rock, Arizona, headquarters of
the Navajo nation, an immense red-rock arch shaped like a
portal rises up above the sandstone buildings that house
tribal offices and the federal Bureau of Indian Affairs. It is an
awesome natural sight; but in the spring of 1992 it was not
possible to get near it because a television commercial was
being filmed in front of it. Surrounded by lights, reflectors, a
camera, a microphone boom, and about a dozen crew members in T-shirts and jeans, a Navajo stood with the rock for-
mation rising up behind him. A handsome old man,
wrinkled from years in the sun, he was wearing a velvet
blouse and a spectacular display of Navajo silver and
turquoise necklaces. The camera crew had recruited him for
his noble appearance; and he looked into the camera and
spoke in a voice that quivered with wisdom and portent. He
delivered his line over and over again, perhaps three dozen
times, until he said it exactly the way the director wanted.
"In nature, all things are balanced," the red man repeated,
each time holding up a perfumed loofah sponge you can
buy at your favorite department store.

We asked one of the crew members about the commercial
being filmed. He explained that the concept was to empha-
size the sponge's closeness to the earth. An Indian was chosen to deliver the message, he said, because "They're more
in touch with nature than anybody else."

ALGERIA

LIBYA

EGYPT

MALI

NIGER

CHAD

BROADCAST NEWS

NIGERIA

SUDAN

IVORY
COAST

ZAIRE

South Atlantic

ANGOLA

IKECHUKWU ACHEBE

ZAMBIA

NAMIBIA

ZIMBABWE

BOTSWANA

SWAZILAND

Ikechukwu Achebe was born in Lagos, Nigeria. He received a bachelor's degree from the University of Kent, Canterbury, England, and a master's degree from Coventry University, England.

Mr. Achebe is a contributing editor for *Okike: An African Journal of New Writing*. He edited and published *Poets in Their Youth: An Anthology of New Nigerian Poetry*, and is the author of *The Historical Imagination in African Literature* and *The Divinity in Numbers: A Cybernetic Analysis of the Computer and Divination*. He was a producer at the Nigerian Television Authority from 1986 to 1990.

Mr. Achebe currently lives in Annandale-on-Hudson, New York.

In the transition from traditional village to global village a battle of cultures is being waged, with icons and symbols as foot soldiers. On every continent, old icons are being replaced by new symbols. The European Economic Community with its new flag, parliament, and exchange rate mechanism, is one example of how the traditional functions of the nation-state are being usurped by newer economic and political alliances.

The history of Nigeria's contact with the West has been a chronicle of convulsion and change. The Nigerian people, like other peoples in Africa, Asia, and Latin America, have been called upon repeatedly to make concessions on almost every aspect of their culture. In most cases, the introduction of Western ideas, products, and habits has resulted in a direct assault on traditional, social, and religious practices. In other cases the process of cultural exchange has been equitable, even mutually beneficial, involving a modification of both the foreign and the indigenous. But in every instance, from the adoption of foreign religions to the introduction of industrial methods, Nigerians have had to look to their own traditions for models of how to cope with the challenges of change. One model on which they have been able to draw comes from the Igbo people, in an ancient form of mud sculpture known as *mbari*.

Mbari is an archival record of the major events and cultural influences that have been witnessed in the community. Every significant episode of the past century in Igboland—the arrival of European missionaries in the nineteenth century, the institution of British colonial administration in Nigeria in 1914, the great influenza epidemic of 1918, the introduction of the telegraph and the motor car, and the inauguration of television—has been intimately depicted and preserved in the molded pieces of *mbari*.

To describe the painstaking artistic endeavor called *mbari* simply as "sculpture" is misleading; for *mbari* is actually an architectural triumph. It is an imposing roofed gallery peopled by scores of mud figurines depicting scenes from everyday life, phantasmagoric figments of the artists' own imaginations, and even strange, unaccustomed icons of foreign cultures, all executed in a highly ornate and colorful style. No one is certain just how old the practice is, but the etymology of *mbari* is instructive and indicates a very old pedigree. It has been variously translated as "festal" or "celebration," the stems *mba* and *eri* suggesting a form of communal feasting that accords with the festive spirit in which the entire enterprise is undertaken.

Mbari, like many religious activites in traditional Igbo society, is regulated by a patron deity, Ani, goddess of the Earth. Ani represents the life-giving principle of the universe and the regenerative qualities of the land. She is the symbol of both justice and retribution and is given pride of place at the head of the most important ritual ceremonies. It is Ani who demands that *mbari* be built, and it is to Ani that the finished project is dedicated.

When tragedy occurs in an Igbo community in the form of violent or unaccountable death or in the outbreak of disease, it is interpreted as a sign that an infraction against the Earth has occurred. The priest of Ani is consulted, and through divination he ascertains the reason for the misfortune—displeasure of the gods, dereliction of ritual duty—and prescribes a suitable satisfaction to cleanse the land. Every so often, however, the evil involved or the offense committed is of a sufficiently grave nature that Ani demands *mbari* as sacrifice. It is then that the great communal effort in construction, purification, and consecration is begun. The priest, again through oracle, selects men and women from each household in the community. They enter two years of seclusion behind a walled enclosure, where they serve as the ritual workers, artisans, and acolytes of *mbari*.

Mbari is an expression of a community's collective consciousness. The artisans who work the red tensile clay are rarely the professional sculptors and craftsmen of the village. Selected entirely at random, they represent the everyday men and women of the farm, marketplace, or school. The molded figures they produce are usually amateurish in execution, but bold and daring in subject matter. They range from models of domestic life (a family at meal) to the dreaded (a man ravaged by measles) to the miraculous (a woman giving birth) to the taboo. No bounds are placed on the artistic imagination. Indeed taboo images are a great favorite with *mbari* artists, appearing among the clay figures to shock and delight spectators.

Mbari artists readily acknowledge that within the creative process itself, in the magic of kneading inchoate matter into form, lies the capacity to restore harmony where disruption has occurred. Thus when members of a community or outside influences create profound strife within Igbo culture, *mbari* artists, by capturing the familiar and foreign elements of the known world in models of ritual clay, aim to rededicate the forces of potential crisis to the greater will of the community and so contain the crisis. The sympathetic magic of *mbari* is really a desire to regain harmony and a mechanism of control; its lesson is not exclusion but the inclusion of all that is new and foreign in a collective effort to preserve order and cohesion in society.

When the American-based Cable News Network began beaming its signals to the Nigerian capital, Lagos, in the early months of 1993, the arrangement was a relatively easy, mutually profitable, affair. For the price of nine hours of air-time, an indigenous company was to broadcast CNN into the homes of the Nigerian viewing public via the channels of the Nigerian Television Authority, a vast

government monopoly and mouthpiece of the military junta that came to power in 1985.

The initial reaction of Nigerians to the development was mixed; on the one hand CNN afforded an alternative to the largely lackluster and propagandist news bulletin of national television; on the other hand it represented the worst aspects of what its detractors came to call cultural imperialism.

During the Cold War, Nigeria had been a member of the Nonaligned Movement, a league of nations formed in 1955 to guarantee the independence of countries that refused to join either the North Atlantic Treaty Organization (NATO) or the Soviet-led Warsaw Pact. Most of the members of the Nonaligned Movement were newly independent states of Africa and Asia; emerging as they were from colonial dominion, they were reluctant to form new alliances with the United States or the Soviet Union.

With the advantage of neutrality, Nigeria had received nationalist propaganda and news dispatches from both superpowers and was able to balance the ideological perspectives of one against those of the other. With the breakup of the Communist bloc, however, the scales shifted and the United States became the single dominant power in the world.

Throughout the cold war, American news media continued to gloss over the unpleasant aspects of United States policy in Africa and around the world. America's policy of "constructive engagement" with the racist government in South Africa before 1986 and its support for the UNITA* rebels led by Jonas Savimbi in Angola were viewed with outrage by many Nigerians.

During the Gulf War, the American consulate in Kaduna, a city in Muslim northern Nigeria, was attacked by Nigerians opposed to the American military campaign in Iraq. And by

---

*UNITA—National Union for the Total Independence of Angola.

the time CNN began its broadcast to Nigeria in 1993, it was already regarded as a particularly potent symbol of the United States and of American interests.

Doubts increased over the wisdom of continuing to allow Nigerians to be bombarded with images from alien perspectives. Many Nigerian academics and businesspeople opposed the CNN broadcasts. This position was supported by a number of unsolicited, dubious groups, many of which stood to gain substantial financial advantage by the collapse of the deal. The managers of Nigerian television, on their part, defended their decision at every turn on grounds of sound economics and good programming, insisting that the policy kept well within the legally stipulated ratio of foreign programs.

And then, as suddenly as it had appeared, CNN disappeared from the screen.

No one now will say why the arrangement was scrapped or on whose instruction. But a series of developments in subsequent months created a sense of hostile suspicion over the intentions of Nigeria's military leaders toward the news media, both foreign and domestic, and toward opponents of the government. That the views of those who really matter—the vast majority of Nigerians, who continued to welcome CNN—were never sought is now of no consequence. Of greater moment were the growing repression and persecution that became the hallmark of the military dictatorship. Since the fiasco with CNN, the illegal detention of journalists and pro-democracy activists by agents of the government has grown. The June 1993 national elections, which were to herald a new era of democratic government, were canceled, and the candidate who many believe would have won was forced into exile. In August a peaceful antigovernment rally was ruthlessly suppressed by the army, and three of the oldest newspapers in the country were raided and sealed off and their editors driven underground by the secret police. All the while the military junta has continued to dismiss as "neocolonialist propaganda" the widespread condemnation of the persecution that has been justly expressed in the Western press.

Like CNN, other champions of the new global enterprise will doubtless come up against resistance in the name of national sovereignty and noninterference. Some of these claims will be based on genuine concern over the pernicious effects that cultural imperialism can have on local traditions and cultures; others will be little more than the self-serving pretext of dictators for whom nothing but a stranglehold on the press will do. The experience of CNN in Nigeria has made that clear.

The many well-meaning Nigerians from academia and business who came out against CNN do not support censorship or oppose foreign programming: There are already a number of foreign programs on Nigerian television. But they do recognize the dangers of a one-sided exchange with America. They insist that for the process of cultural diffusion to work it must be akin to the idea of technology transfer, which is most successful when the imported technology is tailored to its new surroundings. Ultimately the argument hinges on the familiar precepts of ancient *mbari* philosophy. It is already a demand by Nigerians, as members of the new global village, that the icons of any new relationship be adapted to the Nigerian milieu; that they included in the international dialogue for mediating and controlling new and potentially disruptive forces in their own country before they become sources of dissension. If as a result of their opposition to CNN these well-meaning Nigerians have unwittingly become implicated in the military's ruthless destruction and repression of the so-called symbols of neocolonialist interference, it is all the more regrettable, and reveals both the difficulty of their position and the complexity of the issue.

Those nations left behind in the process, the developing countries that remain obdurately in the intermediate stage between old and new, will find that they have been overtaken by developments. In the forging of new alliances, the symbol of *mbari* as a metaphor of cohesion will have to be invoked to aid the reconciliation of conflicting notions, interests, and icons. Uncontrolled cultural diffusion with its attendant danger of cultural imperialism is as undesirable as the iron curtain of exclusion with its capacity for repression and dictatorship.

That is the lesson of *mbari*.

THE LAUGHTER OF
HEROES

JONATHAN NEALE

J onathan Neale was born in the United States. He has lived in London for the past twenty years, where he works as a counselor at an HIV education center.

The following selection is an excerpt from his forthcoming book *The Laughter of Heroes*, to be published by Serpents Tail in November.

In any other country it would have been a cheap hotel room. In China there are no cheap rooms for tourists. The thin Englishman doesn't have much money left. He is traveling on his own, not part of any tour. The clerk is polite, and there is a jug of water and a clean glass on the bedside table. The thin Englishman takes the room and signs the register: John Parsons. He feels tired and goes straight to bed. The next morning he goes out for a walk around the town. When he comes back to the room at first everything looks the same.

An hour later John is desperately sorting through his belongings. He stuffs everything back in the rucksack for the third time. Then he tears his things out again, spilling them across the bed: the *Tibetan Book of the Dead*, some yellow boxer shorts he used to think were trendy, his red socks, the *Lonely Planet Guide to Tibet*, his toothbrush, three hand puppets, a prayer wheel. It is not there. He suddenly has trouble with his breathing. He tells himself it is only panic. His hands rummage through the corners of the rucksack, tear around in the things on the bed.

There is a knock on the door. John freezes. His body stiff, he turns his face slowly toward the door. He is thirty-nine but looks older. He has recently grown a blond beard. Sweat stands out on his cheekbones. He stares at the door and his eyes lose focus. There is a noise on the other side of the door. John begins to shake. Then he understands. The noise is footsteps moving away from the door. John sits down on the bed and recites a mantra under his breath. He gets control of his legs and his lungs. Then it comes to him—under the bed.

John gets down under the bed, awkwardly pulling himself forward with his elbows. He finds one shoe. It is a man's shoe of Western manufacture, recently polished and not cheap. It is a large size. John has small feet for a man of almost six feet. Who left it? Why only one shoe?

He never finds out. The doorknob turns behind him, and two men step silently into the room. Each cradles a small gun in his fist.

John's legs stick out from under the bed toward the door. The older man signals for the younger to cover the door. Then he glides across to the other side of the room and bends down.

John sees a face and a gun framed by the bed. He screams.

"Lost something?" the face asks.

"No," John says.

"I rather think you have," the face says. The voice is Oxbridge, the face Chinese. That scares John as much as anything. John says nothing.

"The reason I think you have," the face says, "is that we have found it."

"You searched my room," John says, trying for an outraged Amnesty International voice.

"It is our duty," the face says. The phrase tells John who they are. The gun motions for John to rise. He scrambles out backward and stands up, conscious of the dust on his shirt. He sees the younger man's gun trained on him. The man wears rubber gloves. John knows what that means.

"Here it is," the older man says. He hands John a small ornamental wooden box. The older man wears gloves too. There is a heron carved on the top of the box. John opens the box to check.

"They are all there," the older man says. Where does his accent come from? Have "we" trained him? "We are not thieves," the man says.

John opens the box anyway. It's all there. He goes over to the bedside table and pours a glass of water. He spills a little. He takes something out of the black box. The younger man grunts and moves forward as if to stop him. The older man says something in National Language. The younger man steps back. The older man says in English: "Be my guest."

John swallows the pill, then the water. The secret policemen watch. The older one says, "You should have told us you had AIDS."

They deport him the same day. He gets through the office in nothing flat, tearing past waiting rooms full of resentful people. The cops all wear rubber gloves and all carry guns. They are polite and careful and they do not look at him. They put him on an airliner.

The pilot's voice comes over the intercom. "Please extinguish all cigarettes and fasten seat belts," the pilot says in English. John remembers that all pilots know English. It is the international language for air traffic control. John doesn't smoke anymore, so he just fastens his seat belt.

"OK," he shouts. No response. Louder: "Fastened."

"Thank you," the intercom says. There seems to be nobody else on the plane.

But after they take off a stewardess appears. Cabin crew, John reminds himself: Stewardess is sexist. She walks down the aisle carrying a tray. John remembers that he has not eaten for twenty-four hours. She wears rubber gloves and a surgeon's paper mask.

She stands a little distance away. John lowers the small plastic table in front of his seat. She holds out the tray.

She is not close enough. He reaches for the tray but it's beyond his fingers. She bends forward from the waist. Still not close enough. He smiles at her. It looks like she's nerving herself to step forward. Then her mask slips off and she jumps back.

John is hungry, so he undoes his seat belt slowly and carefully. As he does so, he keeps looking at her with a gentle expression. She has pasted a smile on her face. It's one of those smiles Oriental stewardesses always wear in the telly ads.

He stands up carefully and reaches out both hands. She

69

makes a little lurch forward and he has the tray. John sits down with his trophy. She stands there; she doesn't seem to know what to do. John doesn't look at her. She turns and begins to wobble back up the aisle. He takes the cover off his food.

"Hey," he shouts at her back. "This isn't vegetarian."

She turns. "No vegetarian," she says.

"I'm a vegetarian," John yells.

"Nobody told me vegetarian." She is crying.

They look at each other down the aisle. She's really blubbering now. "Nobody told me," she says. "Is only one meal."

"I'll eat the vegetables," he says, fast, feeling guilty. He reaches for the spoon and begins shoveling cabbage. "See, I'm eating the vegetables."

"I am sorry," she says.

"It's OK. I'll eat the vegetables. I'll just leave the meat. It's no problem. Really."

He eats quickly to show his appreciation.

She stands looking at him. She seems friendly, but she doesn't come any closer. Her makeup is a mess.

"I'm sorry I yelled," John says. "It's just that I've never been deported before."

In a small voice she says, "I have never deport before either."

John makes himself smile. She smiles back and sniffles.

"You want in-flight movie?" she asks.

A week later, back home in London, John's father and sister come over to visit. He takes them for a walk on Hampstead Heath. It is a spring day in 1990. The Berlin Wall came down the year before, but John Major is not Prime Minister yet and EuroDisney is still a building site. The weather is beautiful: clear, sunny, and still a bit cold. It rained last night.

"I should have worn my welly boots," his sister Claire

says to herself. She is thirty-five, and her reddish brown hair bounces on her shoulders. She is wearing one of her uncompromising green Peruvian ponchos. When she was a teenager she used to go around wearing a blanket with a hole cut in it for her head. John likes her.

"You managing all right?" John asks his father. Bill's wife, John and Claire's mother, died in November.

"Yes," Bill says.

"You're lying, Dad," Claire says.

"I get down to the pub for a pint and a natter most nights," Bill says. He walks with his back held carefully straight. John remembers his father is seventy. Bill's hair is white, and he still has most of it. John is grateful for inheriting a full head of hair.

Bill changes the subject. "How was China?" he asks John.

"OK," John says.

"Just OK?" Claire asks. She is heavily into acupuncture.

"Just OK," John says. He can't tell Dad about the deportation. He will tell Claire later when they're alone.

"I thought you were going to love China," Claire says.

"So did I," John says.

"What happened?" Claire says. There's no stopping her.

"Too many secret policemen," John mumbles.

"I thought they were moving away from communism," Bill says.

John feels trapped. "It's not because they're communist," he says. "Thatcher loves the butchers of Tiananmen Square."

"She's done quite a lot of good for this country," Bill says. He voted Liberal last time himself, but you have to be fair.

"You promised," Claire reminds John. He has promised not to get into political arguments with Dad.

"I didn't mention Thatcher," John says. "He did." This is not strictly true.

"I don't agree with Tiananmen Square either," Claire says firmly. "But they do have a big country to govern."

"A big country," John sneers. He must stop this.

"A billion people," she says. "That's not easy to control."

"Control?" John yelps. He can't stop. "Control? That's elitist. Is that what they taught you at Milton Keynes?" Claire did her acupuncture studies in Milton Keynes.

Claire doesn't like being called elitist. "Leamington Spa," she says.

"Leamington Spa," John says. Claire did her acupuncture studies in Leamington Spa.

"Nice town, Leamington Spa," Bill says. He can't stand to see his children fighting.

"No," Claire says, "they didn't."

"Really lovely eighteenth-century parade," Bill says.

"Yes, Dad," Claire says, "it is."

John's legs buckle and he falls onto the wet grass.

Next day John is tucked up in bed at his flat in Tufnell Park. The worst is over. Most of his puppets are in the big trunk in the corner. Big Ted and Andy the Mouse, his hand puppet, are in the bed with him. On the bedroom wall are framed pictures of John in his working dinner-jacket with his favorite puppets. He is alive. Claire ranges back and forth at the foot of the bed, throwing her arms around for emphasis. She is wearing a red poncho today. It sets off her hair.

"Why don't you tell him?" she says.

"Who?" John says.

"You're being deliberate."

"Dad," he admits.

"Yes," Claire says, her right arm chopping air, "Dad."

"I don't think it would be a good idea," John says.

"You don't think it would be a good idea."

"No," he says, "I don't think he'd handle it very well."

"You don't think he'd handle it very well." Claire used

to repeat his sentences the same way when they were kids and she wanted to wind him up.

"You remember how he was when I came out," John says.

"Yes," she says. She strides around to stand next to him. "You told him you were a ho-mo-sex-u-al, and he was a bastard."

"Yes," John says.

"And now you're punishing him," she says.

"I'm not punishing him. He hasn't got over Mum yet. I don't want him worrying about me."

"You're punishing him," Claire says. She puts her fists on her hips and frowns down at him. "And don't use Mum to manipulate me."

John pulls the covers up to his neck and shrinks under them. "You gotta be nice to me," he whines. "I'm sick."

"Balls," Claire says. He likes his sister.

Next day John is a bit better, but not that much. He lives alone in a housing association flat on the top two floors of a house, in Tufnell Park. Last time John got sick, his friends took turns looking after him. Paul, Mark, Babur, and Keith were the main ones. They developed a sort of regimental spirit about it, and started calling themselves the Firm. Claire took her turns too, but never really felt she was part of the Firm. They were careful to try to include her, of course. But she sensed something: maybe that they had to try.

Claire sits in the open window of John's kitchen, a cup of jasmine tea warming her hands. It is the nicest place in the house, thirty feet above the garden. She looks out over the back gardens of John's quiet neighbors. She feels a little spurt of anger over the great trees pollarded down to gray stumps. But on one side there is a greenhouse and vegetables, and on the other side an army of chickens peck over the brown dirt. Beyond them is a row of pines, and then the backs of more houses. Claire looks up the hill to the skyline, the great slab of the Dark Tower where the social security people lurk and the green Byzantine dome of the Catholic Church on Highgate Hill.

It's time to call in the Firm again. Claire phones Paul. He's the one who organizes things. Paul calls Mark and Babur's number. Babur answers and promises to tell Mark when he gets in. When Mark gets home, Babur tells him, and Mark calls Keith, the last of the Firm.

The Firm arrange to meet at John's place at nine that night.

Paul gets to John's half an hour early. Claire lets him in. Paul needs the time to set up his chart. Last time they had a bit of difficulty organizing the rota. The uncertainty got to Paul. So he stole a big A2 flipchart from work, and that sorted everything out. Paul put their names down one side and the days across the top. They took turns at day and night shifts. So Paul had a big blue felt marker for days and a red one for nights. Then all Paul had to do was put a tick under the right person's name in the right color for their shift. They could put the sheet up on the wall of John's living room with Blu-Tack and anybody could see his next shift at a glance. Paul plans to use the same system this time. He sets it up in the living room. John is already asleep in his bedroom upstairs.

They sort out the day shifts pretty quickly. Nights are more of a problem. Keith can't do Wednesdays because of his union meeting. Paul asks the room, "How about Thursday nights?"

"Thursdays is my Poll Tax meeting," Keith says very fast.

"I'll do Thursdays," Paul says, and puts a tick by his name.

"I can do Saturday nights," Keith says.

"You sure?" Paul asks. Keith nods. Sometimes Paul puts

a tick next to Keith's name, and then Keith remembers a meeting or changes his mind or something. Then Paul has to get the Tipp-Ex out and change everything round, but it never really looks right. Paul puts a tick next to Keith's name.

Keith mumbles. Paul checks him. Keith is looking at his Filofax. Where's the Tipp-Ex?

They work it all out for the next weeks, even though it turns out Paul has forgotten the Tipp-Ex.

A week later Paul is cooking supper. John feels better, so he comes down to sit at the kitchen table and chat. John has a tendency to tell other people how to cook. A lot of good cooks are like that. Paul got used to it when they lived together.

"Why don't you tell him?" Paul says, wiping the counter top.

"Tell who?" John says.

"John," Paul says firmly in his don't-give-me-that voice.

"My dad?" John says.

"Your dad," Paul says. He reaches up and takes the oregano off the spice rack.

"Oregano?" John sounds surprised.

"Yes," Paul says.

"On chops?"

"No?" Paul says.

"Sometimes," John says.

What the hell does that mean, sometimes? "Don't change the subject," Paul says.

John moves his coffee cup around the table in a small circle. "Did Claire put you up to this?"

"Yes." Paul smiles.

"I don't want to tell him," John says.

"You'll feel better." Paul doesn't know why he says this. He does not believe it.

"You remember how he acted when I came out?" John

75

has his debating face on.

"No," Paul says. He can't decide what to make for pudding.

"I told you," John says.

"I mean I wasn't there," Paul says. Tinned fruit cocktail and custard, maybe.

"I told him. I gathered up all my courage and went home and we went for a walk and I just told him. Know what he said?"

Paul does not want to interrupt the flow. He puts the chops under the grill.

"He said . . ." John pauses to go into his father's voice. It still amazes Paul how John can do voices. It's being a puppeteer, of course. "Daffodils are a bit late this year. I can't figure it out: The crocuses came right on time."

"That's the greenhouse effect," Paul says.

"He was denying me," John snaps. "That was denial."

"And now you're punishing him," Paul says.

"The bastard didn't mention it again. Ever again," John says. His fingers are clenched around his coffee cup. There is a picture of Garfield on the cup. Garfield smiles like an idiot.

"He tries," Paul says.

"He couldn't handle it."

Paul checks the chops. OK.

"He couldn't handle Mum, he couldn't handle me," John says.

"He is going to find out eventually." Paul hates saying this, but it needs saying. "How's he going to feel then?"

"Maybe he'll peg out first," John says.

Now Paul turns from the cooking and looks directly into John's blue eyes. His friend looks stricken. "I didn't mean that," John says.

"It's OK," Paul says. He thinks, also it's true.

"I'm not punishing him," John says. He sounds seven years old. "I'm not." His eyes are watery. Paul feels like a bastard.

"I'm sorry," Paul says. He wants to put his arm around John's shoulder. Very badly. He thinks John would not like it. He does not know if John would like it. He could not bear it if John shrugged off his arm.

John puts his face down on the table, his arms pulled round to hide it. He talks quietly. "When we were kids, I was ten, Claire was five, Dad promised to take us to Disneyland. I've never been so happy. I told everybody in school, weeks before. I got a special mouse hat. I loved that hat. It had good ears. We went to the airport, I'd never been on a plane before, we were going to America—we got to the airport and—nothing. Dad wouldn't get on the plane. He just sat. He wouldn't talk to me. We all just sat there like Mickey Mouse was dead or something, and then we got on the train and went back home and didn't say anything to each other, and all the kids at school thought I'd made the whole thing up. To look important." He looks up at Paul, his face blubbery. "I've never wanted anything that much in my life."

The chops are on fire.

John sleeps like a baby all night. Paul does not. He is too excited by his new idea. Next morning is Saturday. Paul is up at six, cleaning and whistling.

Keith arrives an hour early because he feels guilty about not doing as much as Paul. Both Paul and Keith have been careful and polite to each other all week. Paul hears the key in the door and greets Keith with a big silly smile as he comes through the door. "We're going to Disneyland," Paul says.

"Disneyland?" Keith says. He needs a cup of coffee.

"Yes." Paul's eyes are shining. "The Florida one. They didn't have it then, but it's cheaper to get to and just as good."

"Coffee?" Keith asks.

Paul stops. "I'm not making much sense, am I?"

"No," Keith says.

So they go into the kitchen and Keith makes some real coffee. Paul tells him about how John never got to go to Disneyland when he was little, and all his life John's wanted to go, and Paul's decided that the one thing they have to do for him is to take him to Disneyland. Soon.

"How soon?" Keith asks. The coffee is waking him up.

"Three weeks," Paul says. He has worked it all out.

"Why three weeks?"

"It has to be soon." Paul tries to explain why with the expression of his face. He does not want to say the words out loud.

"I can't get off school," Keith says.

"Oh." Paul hadn't thought about that side of things. As far as Paul is concerned, if his company get antsy, they can stay antsy.

"We only get holidays at half-terms and summer," Keith says.

"Like kids?" Paul says.

"Like kids. We get the same holidays they do."

Paul leans back against the cupboards. He looks deflated. He tries so hard, Keith thinks. So Keith says, "It sounds like a good idea."

"Do you think so?"

"A cracker," Keith says. He wiggles his eyebrows. "Wicked."

Paul cheers up and straightens. "We'll have to keep it secret," he says.

"Why?" Keith asks. With Paul it's never going to be simple.

"So it's a surprise," Paul says. "It's John's birthday in two weeks."

Right. "Who's we?" Keith asks.

"The Firm."

Keith feels included. It feels good. "I'll try to get the time off," he says.

"Try," Paul says. "It won't be the same without you."

Paul leaves John's flat and decides to walk to Mark and Babur's. It's a half-hour walk, but Paul is buzzing with energy. He cuts across Whittington Park, smiling benignly at the dogs, toddlers, and drinkers. He turns up the Holloway Road, with its row of pubs for men a long way from home. Gresham's Ballroom advertises another Irish country and western singer, his pink face smiling over a shirt with mother-of-pearl buttons. In the window of the Freethinkers store the anti-God pamphlets are still curling at the edges. Paul read somewhere they keep going on a bequest from George Bernard Shaw.

Mark and Babur's house is a row set back from the Archway Road, just before suicide bridge. The grass grows high and the gardens wild in front of these houses, and some of the houses have slogans painted on the wall. Their flat is warm, messier than Paul could live with, throw rugs and kelims everywhere. Paul settles on a red and black cushion. He tells them the plan.

"Oh, wow," Babur says. "Yes." He claps his hands. Mark watches him. That's one of the things Mark loves about Babur. He's so damn affirmative. Mark cannot understand what somebody like Babur sees in a depressive like him.

"Gee, isn't that great," Babur is saying. "Disneyland."

Paul smiles. "Disney World really, but I'm sure it will be just as good, and there's a lot less pollution than in Los Angeles."

"Just as good," Babur says. "Definitely. I'm going to get some of those awful checked shorts. The ones that come down to the knees."

Paul leans forward and pantomimes looking around. "We have to keep it a secret," he says. "We can't tell anybody till John's birthday."

"I love secrets," Babur says.

Mark does not like secrets. He hated the closet. He is a counselor. He works at bringing old family secrets into the light of day and blowing them away like ancient skeletons. Mark has recently finished writing a paper on the harmful effects of secrets in families.

"I think I like secrets even more than chocolate," Babur says.

"I love them too," Paul says.

It is everything Mark can do to keep his mouth shut.

"And I'm going to get some of those reflecting sunglasses," Babur says, "like the pimps wear, and the cops, the American cops with the cattle prods dangling off their belts. I'm going to be real menacing." Babur sticks out his chin. He stands up and starts threatening Paul with an imaginary cattle prod.

Paul laughs.

Over his shoulder, including Mark in the fun, Babur asks, "What are you going to get, love?"

Mark might as well say it now. "I don't think I'm going to be able to get the time off."

"You have to. The whole Firm has to go," Paul says.

"I can't just drop my patients." Mark knows he's supposed to call them clients, but somehow he keeps calling them patients.

"Of course not," Babur says over his shoulder. His face has gone hard now, no longer childlike. Babur is twenty-eight. "You're the therapist." Mark had forgotten Babur was a porter and had this thing about class. Mark feels guilty.

"Keith's really mad keen to go," Paul says from his cushion on the floor.

Mark holds his hands out to Babur, justifying himself. "They need me. I make contracts with them. It matters that I'm there every week right when I said I would be."

"Half the time they don't turn up," Babur says.

"It still matters," Mark says. "They need to know I'm

there. They need the order in their lives. Some of them are very frightened people." This is true.

"You're indispensable," Babur says.

"I know I'm not indispensable," Mark says. This is a lie.

"Keith and Babur and me all want to go." Paul knows he sounds overeager. What the hell. He is overeager.

Babur's face lights up again. "Leave him to me," he says. Babur flashes his impossibly white teeth.

Two in the morning, and John lies in bed in the dark. The sheets are soaked. He's been sweating again. The night sweats frightened him at first. Then he read somewhere that heavy sweating is how the body expels poisons it can't get rid of in any other way. That's why the sweat smells awful: It's the poison. Heavy smokers sweat at night, and drinkers, and people with HIV. John finds this comforting. His body is doing what it can.

But now he's awake and he can't get back to sleep. He doesn't want to call Paul up from downstairs. He'd come bounding in, worried and guilty and solicitous. And right now John is not sick. He just has insomnia.

It's a double bed. Andy lies on the other pillow. Andy the Mouse is a puppet, and John is a puppeteer. He started out making them. Now it is mainly performing, though he still makes a few of his own. He did buy a couple of new ones in China. It's not a very secure way to make a living, but he has always liked puppets. Andy is a hand puppet, and John's favorite. When he can't sleep, he talks to Andy.

"Can't sleep, huh?"

Andy can't sleep.

"Don't worry," John says. "No problem. Be happy."

Andy is still worried.

John talks softly in the dark. "Up in the mountains, in the High Himalayas, beyond Kashmir, there is a valley called Zanskar. They threw us out of China before we got to Tibet." Andy does not like remembering that bit. "But

81

Zanskar, in the olden days it was part of the Kingdom of the Sikhs, and the Sikhs called it Little Tibet. The people up there speak a Tibetan dialect, and in the high pastures along the border the nomads still live in their black tents with their yaks. The air is clear and the mountains are pyramids of crystal glass. First you come to Dardistan, the land of the fairies, and beyond those mountains is Zanskar. And I've got tickets."

He feels in the drawer of his bedside table and brings out the tickets. Really there is only one ticket. Andy can travel free in John's bag. Nobody knows John talks to his mouse like this. He does not bother to turn on the bedside lamp. Andy can't read.

"Here they are. Tickets to Srinagar in Kashmir. We don't have to tell anybody. As soon as I'm over this bit, we'll just melt away in the fog one morning and send everybody postcards. They might worry, you know. Might try to stop us."

John got the ticket in a bucket shop the day after he came back from China. It was cheap, one-way.

"They have a monastery there, one of those high-sided adobe ones, like a Spanish fantasy, tiny windows high up, built into the side of the rock, and the monks sit there and sing their prayers all day. They'll have flickering butter lamps and orange robes and those great musical horns. We'll find peace there."

Andy has drifted off to sleep.

John has his first truly good day for two months. The itch in his armpits is still there, and the rash on his bits and pieces. But his body feels good now, almost . . .

He stretches. He loves the dreamy moment when you surface from a nap.

He wants to run through the autumn leaves holding hands. He wants to throw snowballs. He wants somebody to take him in their arms and say, follow me to the gates of joy. He wants a cup of coffee. He is getting better.

He gets out of bed and scrabbles into a sweatshirt and trousers. He opens his bedroom door. At the top of the stairs some sixth sense alerts him. He bends over, peers down.

"Surprise," they yell up at him.

It's wonderful. They have chocolate ice cream, and butter pecan ice cream, and one of those Sara Lee chocolate gateaux, the kind you get all over your hands. John is in small boy heaven.

He looks around the room. They're all there. Keith, Paul, Mark, Babur, Claire. This has Paul written all over it. Well organized, done with love, he's remembered all John's favorite foods. And yes, there are the plastic forks and plates. When they lived together Paul had explained the merits of plastic entertaining. Some people thought plastic plates were tacky, but if you used the real thing once you got over a certain number, you just had endless mess afterward. And if you had paper plates people put them down on the floor, inevitably, somebody got drunk and put their plate on the floor, they were probably thinking about something else, and then the beet juice or the goo or whatever, soaked through the paper plate and onto the carpet and you never, never got it out. And that sort of thing could wreck a whole party for Paul. Just worrying about its maybe happening could wreck a whole party.

John looks around for Paul. Somebody has lit the candles. John counts. Forty. All his years. Little pink candles. The political touch. They're all singing:

"— to You
Happy Birthday to You
Happy Birthday to John,"
(and a crashing)
"Happy Birthday to You,"
And a ragged cheer.

"Thank you," John says.

Paul hands him a small glass. He sniffs the liquid. Cointreau. Paul. "Damn the pills," John says, and knocks it back.

He sits in front of the cake.

"Make a wish," Claire says. All his life she's said that. He makes a wish. He keeps it to himself. Nobody ever finds out what John's birthday wishes are. He sucks everything into his lungs and gets all the candles in one blow. That means the wish will come true within the year. They clap.

Paul is standing in front of him with an envelope. This seems formal. They're going to give him a gold watch. Paul coughs officially. Yes, definitely a gold watch.

"From Claire and the Firm," Paul says. He hands John the envelope. It's a card or something. John opens it. Everybody watches. It takes him a minute to realize what it is. An airline ticket. He cannot speak. He's so happy. Tibet. How did they know? He holds the ticket in his left hand. He looks up at Paul. He knows his eyes are shiny.

"It's for Disneyland," Claire says.

Damn.

"We're all taking you to Disneyland," Paul says. "It's a ticket for Miami."

John can feel the love in John's voice. John knows his feelings must be showing on his face. He must control it. Damn, damn, damn. He welds a smile onto his face. He does not want to die in Miami. He makes himself look up at Paul.

"Thank you, love," he says. "It's lovely. It's so sweet of you." And he starts to cry. The others crowd round. John looks at his lap. "Thank you, all of you," he says. "Thank you so much."

Next morning John and Andy are sitting up in bed.

"You want to see the tickets to India?" John asks.

"No," says the puppet.

John sulks.

"You have to go to Disneyland," Andy the Mouse says.

"I don't have to do anything," John says, in the voice of an angry four-year-old.

"I want to see Mickey," Andy says.

"Mickey." John is derisive.

Andy sings, "M-I-C-K-E-Y M-O-U-S-E." He is trying to cheer John up. They sing the chorus together a second time.

"No," John says.

"It's all right for you," Andy says. "I'm a mouse. Do you know how many role models there are for a young mouse? Do you have any idea? And what kind of role models? Mickey built something. Something real. I want to see it."

"You know what Disney did to the workers?" John asks.

"That is not relevant," Andy says firmly.

"Do you?" John asks.

"You're going to tell me anyway."

"He was a fanatic union buster," John lectures the mouse. "Real trade unionism in Hollywood started with the animators' strike at Disney, and Jolly Uncle Walt never forgave them. Hated the CP from then on. Bet you didn't know Snow White was drawn by Communists?"

"You told me before," Andy says.

"Then after the war, Disney and Reagan, he was running the Screen Actors Guild, they ganged up together to feed names to the McCarthy Committee . . ."

"It wasn't McCarthy, it was the House Un-American Activities Committee," the mouse says, "and none of this is relevant. You always get political when you want to avoid things."

John puts on an American gangster voice. "D'ja know Big Ronnie Reagan was an FBI stoolie for years?"

"They're your friends and they love you," Andy says.

"Big deal," John says.

"And they're trying to make you happy, the best they know how."

John collapses back against the pillows. The hand that holds Andy flops onto the bed. They lie there a minute, looking up at the ceiling.

John speaks in a different voice, quiet. "I want to . . . to go to the Himalayas. I want to. It's an empty place, me and the sky. When you die there they put you on a wooden platform below the sky and the vultures come and eat the body. Because you're gone, you've left the body. You continue on and on. Sometimes you come back as a beetle and sometimes a man. Sometimes I guess you're a vulture. It's all one. Because in the end, it sounds silly in words, but we're all one. You have to stop pushing the river: It flows by itself. I don't know what happens, you know I don't. But even if it's just darkness I want that peace. I want some understanding. I've walked through my life, I worked, I loved, I made breakfast. Now I'm concentrated. I want a shape to my life, a form, a meaning." He stares at Andy. "I know it all sounds like crap. But that's what I want, that moment."

They both lie together.

"That moment comes when you're alone," John says.

He is quiet for a while.

"They're your friends, and they're trying to make you happy," Andy says.

"I have to live for myself," John says.

"You have to go," Andy says.

"No."

"What can you do?" Andy asks.

"I can sneak out," John says.

"I wanna see Mickey," Andy says.

"I can still walk," John says.

Andy can never resist an adventure. "Take me with you," he says.

John considers. "OK," he says.

*   *   *

"Come on, John," says Andy the Mouse.

"It's no good," John says. He throws his new "Conan the Barbarian" T-shirt into a lump on the floor.

"Oh, John," Andy says. "It doesn't have to be Tibet. You can merge with ultimate emptiness anywhere. There's ultimate emptiness all around us, if only you know where to look."

"That's all very well," John says, "but what am I going to wear?"

John takes a small pair of wraparound reflecting sunglasses from his bedside table. He places them gently on Andy's face. The mouse chokes back a sob of gratitude. John smiles at him.

"Buddy," Andy says.

"Yeah?"

"Thanks," Andy says.

John produces another pair of reflecting shades, larger, more menacing. John puts them on his own face. They get up and walk over to the mirror on the closet door.

"Dead cool, Kemo Sabe," Andy says.

"Something, huh?" John says.

They admire themselves for a time.

"We're gonna see Mickey," Andy says. John feels happy for the little critter.

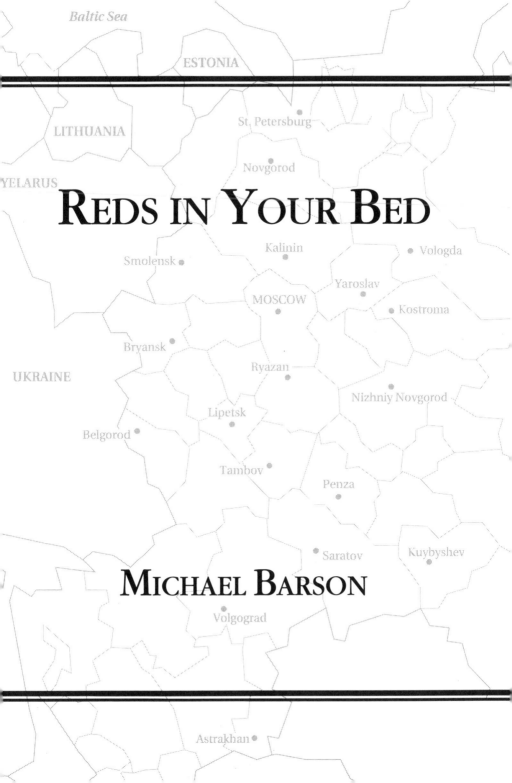

REDS IN YOUR BED

MICHAEL BARSON

Michael Barson was born in Haverhill, Massachusetts. He is the creator of several postcard format books of "B" movie posters, including *Lost, Lonely and Vicious*. He is the author of *Better Dead Than Red* and editor of *Flywheel, Shyster & Flywheel: The Marx Brothers' Lost Radio Show*. His books have been featured on the *Today* show, *Entertainment Tonight*, and in the *New York Times*, *People*, and *The Village Voice*, among others.

Mr. Barson's writing has appeared in *Rolling Stone*, *New York Newsday*, *American Film*, and *Nostalgia*.

Mr. Barson is currently at work on *The Illustrated Who's Who of Hollywood Directors* and *I Married a Monster from Outer Space*, both to be published in fall of 1994. He lives in New Jersey with his wife, Jean Behrend, and sons, Benjamin and Daniel.

America has always been possessed of a phenomenally brief attention span, particularly when some sort of embarrassing behavior on our part seems better off forgotten. What you don't remember can't make you blush. Over the course of two hundred-odd (very odd!) years, we've entered into hostilities with once-and-future allies like the British, the French, the Germans, the Japanese—about half the planet when you get right down to it. And we have always eventually kissed and made up. That's just the kind of lovable, forgiving chumps we are. Look at Mexico: Who remembers the Alamo? Of course, forgetting comes easier after a hundred or so years have gone by. If Saddam Hussein can just be patient . . .

When it comes to the former USSR, however, America has had more than her share of ups and downs and other kinds of reversals. We started off on the wrong foot shortly after the Bolsheviks seized power in November 1917 and the new government was established: When the Bolsheviks pulled Russia out of World War I a few months later to focus their energies on the civil war, the United States and other of Russia's former World War I allies stepped in to assist; unfortunately, we supported the losers, the tsar's anti-Bolshevik forces.

That might have predisposed America to respond over-enthusiastically to the first "Communist offensive." It began with the June 1919 bombing of Attorney General A. Mitchell Palmer's Washington, DC, home—a blast that harmed no one but the inept bomber himself, true, but which turned out to be one of nine set off that evening on the doorsteps of eminent lawmakers across the country. "Plainly of Bolshevik or IWW [Industrial Workers of the World] origin," trumpeted the *New York Times* the next day, and the first Red Scare was underway.

91

Attorney General Palmer went before Congress to solicit a half million dollars for the express purpose of establishing a new task force within the Department of Justice that could investigate and prosecute the hordes of anarchists who had penetrated our midst. The money was appropriated, and the Anti-Radical Division was born. It was headed by a twenty-four-year-old librarian from Justice by the name of J. Edgar Hoover.

Always enterprising, Hoover soon had accumulated a wish list of subversives that boasted an alarming 150,000 names, thanks to the indefatigable research of private detective agencies and local Red Squads—this despite the fact that combined membership of the Communist Party of America and its rival branch, the Communist Labor Party, was generously estimated at 30,000. (It might have been less than half that number, since members who switched from one to the other may have been counted twice.) With the Anti-Radical Division renamed the General Intelligence Division, Hoover and his mentor Palmer conducted raid after raid in 1919 and 1920, netting thousands of befuddled "anarchists" who were promptly deported to Mother Russia on a flotilla of Soviet "Arks."

But it soon became known that most of these arrests were spurious, not to mention completely illegal, and A. Mitchell Palmer's years of glory turned to ashes in his mouth as he was lambasted by the Senate Rules Committee. Palmer's political career was over, and so was the first Red Scare.

But somehow his young protégé escaped a similar fate, going on to be named the first Director of the fledgling Federal Bureau of Investigation in 1924—the same year that Lenin died and Joseph Stalin rose to power, as fate would have it. "Communism is the most evil, monstrous conspiracy against man since time began," Hoover sputtered, but for the moment America had stopped listening.

Through the remainder of the 1920s and much of the

'30s, America remained on a fairly even keel in its response to the Soviet Union. Stalin had already embarked upon what in later years the American media would label his reign of terror, but for the time being his paranoid brutality toward his own people was not known, and his stateside press consisted of generally positive reviews of his visionary leadership. Indeed, for a time the biggest news out of the USSR was that actress Anna Sten had been signed by studio boss Sam Goldwyn to come to Hollywood in 1934 to make motion pictures. She was hoped to be the next Garbo. Although that degree of celebrity never was attained, the fact of her being Russian actually seemed to further her career in its early stages.

But the Moscow Purge Trials of 1937–38 took some of the bloom off this Red rose, and the Hitler-Stalin nonaggression pact of 1939 threw America into the throes of its second Red Scare. *Cosmopolitan* magazine ran a critical article that fall entitled "Stalin: Hitler's New Ally," one of many to appear in the popular press late in 1939. Taking things a step further were *Click* magazine's fanciful photo essays, "The Trojan Horse Policy of Communism in America" in September 1939 and "If the Communists Seized America in 1942" in March 1940, the latter complete with a dramatic illustration of FDR being sentenced to death before a Red tribunal.

These alarmist responses to events in Europe were hardly echoed in Hollywood, which had ignored the first Red Scare entirely and made light of the second one in frothy productions like "Ninotchka" and "Comrade X." Perhaps more substantial, serious motion pictures about these issues would have emerged in time, had not the Hitler-Stalin alliance crumbled after Hitler launched his Operation Barbarossa against the unprepared Soviet Union in June 1941. That act of war put Stalin in bed with Washington, which was suddenly faced with the question of what to do with him. We were not yet participants in the war against Hitler, but if that day came, we wanted the Germans to have an Eastern front as well as a Western front with which to cope, as they had in WWI. At the moment, Stalin needed us more than we needed him—but then came Pearl Harbor, and the level of need suddenly became equal.

And so Making Nice with Marshal Stalin became the order of the day—but by whose orders? While not-for-profit organizations like Russian War Relief were organized to raise money for our ally—one famous photograph featured young crooner Frank Sinatra selling *schmatte* for the cause—FDR helped prepare and on November 6, 1942, signed into law a bill to lend the Russians a billion dollars. This lend-lease fund, as it was called, was interest-free and involved no repayment for ten years. (Of course, ten years later we were locked in a death struggle with the Evil Empire, and presumably that first installment went into permanent arrears.) As headlines in the *New York Times* heralded the triumphs of our new allies—"Nazis' Grip on Stalingrad Broken"; "Russians Break Leningrad Siege; Soviet Gains Grow"— the notion of stirring up popular support for the USSR became a priority with FDR. Years later, Jack Warner of Warner Bros. studio would testify before the House Un-American Activities Committee (HUAC)* that the President had summoned him to a private session, where Warner was instructed to make a film that would excite American moviegoers over Russia's Great Patriotic War. For the Warner Bros. studio, that presidential command (which was, in fact, never verified) translated into the 1943 film "Mission to Moscow," based on the 1941 memoir by former ambassador Joseph E. Davies. A whitewash of gargantuan proportions, it

---

*House Un-American Activities Committee—Established in 1938, it was created to investigate Communist activity in the United States. During World War II, it redirected its energies into anti-Nazi activities. At war's end, it returned to its original assignment.

glossed over the Purge Trials and other of Stalin's nefarious activities from 1936 to 1938. The film was heavily promoted but failed to attract much of an audience. No matter: Jack Warner had done his bit.

Presumably Warner Bros. wasn't the only studio charged with such a mission, assuming Jack Warner wasn't just blowing smoke. Several other pro-Soviet entertainments were released in 1943, among them MGM's glossy (and hilarious) "Song of Russia," United Artists' "Three Russian Girls," Sam Goldwyn's RKO production "The North Star" from a screenplay by Lillian Hellman, 20th Century-Fox's "B" picture "Chetniks! The Fighting Guerrillas" with Anna Sten (who also starred in "Girls") and Columbia's "The Boy From Stalingrad." Not a "Citizen Kane" among them, true; but they had good will to burn. And, without exception, the producers, actors, and screenwriters involved with these films would be roasted on spits before HUAC just a few years later, being asked to explain why they had aided and abetted the enemy. The "FDR Made Me Do It" excuse was withal the most effective, but plenty of other imaginative ones were invoked. Few had the nerve simply to say, *What enemy?* These guys were on *our* side at the time—the President *told* us so!

As 1945 saw the war irreversibly turning in favor of the Allied forces, further forays into pro-Soviet entertainments were notably absent from Hollywood product. But was that because the message in support of the Soviet ally had already been successfully conveyed, or because Washington was rethinking its stand? The Teheran conference of December 1943 between Stalin, Winston Churchill, and FDR had been a public relations success, as had Yalta in February 1945. But just one month after Yalta, Romania had forcibly become a Communist satellite, with Bulgaria falling under Soviet control in September and Albania in December. These were overt violations of the Yalta agreement and served notice to the US and Great Britain that their services were no longer required. But even that sort of effrontery could not completely defuse the American media's conditioned reflex to stroke the image of "Uncle Joe" Stalin. In November 1945, *Look* magazine ran a debate over whether the US should give the USSR the atomic bomb. The experts polled were divided. But late in 1945, the Big Three were still operating under the facade of amicable cooperation. This was evidenced by the *New York Times* headline following the December 29 conference in Moscow attended by each country's foreign minister: "Big Three Reestablish Unity in Wide Accord: Agree on Atom, Treaties, Japan, China, Korea; Unanimity to Rule." As Eddie Haskell of "Leave It to Beaver" would be wont to comment in later times: Yeah, right.

The final break between the US and the Soviet Union is hard to pinpoint, as no single event seemed to precipitate the split. Certainly the symbolic moment must be credited to Sir Winston, who in the spring of 1946 traveled to tiny Westminster College in Missouri and delivered the famed speech that included the galvanizing line, "From Stettin in the Baltic to Trieste in the Adriatic, an iron curtain has descended across the Continent. . . ." The phrase codified the beginning of the Cold War. Despite that, in May 1946, Representative Helen G. Douglas of the House Committee on Foreign Affairs told *Look* magazine, "I cannot believe there is any 'war with Russia' to be avoided. The entire issue which has been raised is a false one, since I cannot believe the Russians want war and I know the American people do not want war." This less than two months after Soviet Ambassador Andrey Gromyko had stormed out of a UN Security Council session to make plain the USSR's refusal to withdraw from Iran.

These Cold War events had little effect upon Hollywood until 1947, when the House Un-American Activities Committee began calling Hollywood's Communist Party members and sympathizers to testify. That noxious scenario has been the subject of entire books, notably Victor Navasky's *Naming Names*. Suffice it to say that the message was conveyed to the studios that it was time to answer for the celluloid wine and roses Hollywood had delivered to Uncle Joe Stalin earlier in the forties. And answer they did, making reparations in the form of such virulent anti-Soviet films as "The Iron Curtain" (Fox), "I Married a Communist" (RKO), "I Was a Communist for the FBI" (Warner Bros.), "My Son John" (Paramount), and "The Red Danube" (MGM). Even studios that hadn't sinned, like Republic, churned out loyalty oaths like "The Red Menace." A few of them even made a little money from this flag-waving. But not much. Self-preservation, not grosses, was the issue that mattered.

The confluence between the US government and the film industry may not have been unique—there were, after all, dozens upon dozens of movies coming out at the same time with overtly patriotic scenarios (sans Russia) that probably were goosed a bit by requests from Washington—but it rarely happened again once WWII reached its conclusion. During the Korean conflict, a number of gung-ho war films were produced, but the sense of urgency that informed the movies from the previous war was absent. As for Vietnam, forget it. John Wayne's "The Green Berets" aside, few if any films overtly set in the midst of that war were made. It is doubtful that Robert Altman's "M*A*S*H" (1970) would have enjoyed its mass success if it had been set in Vietnam instead of Korea, even though most Americans probably got the point.

But while turn about is fair play, never before or since has Hollywood reversed itself so dramatically on an ideological stance—particularly one that was still so popular among the members of its community—as it did when it came to the Soviet Union. But never before had a big stick like HUAC been waved in their faces, and never again would the sort of mass collusion that empowered HUAC find such fertile soil. In the end, both the pro-Soviet propaganda of the war years and the anti-Soviet movies from the first brushfire of the Cold War would recede into obscurity, their transparent moralizing of little interest to latter-day audiences once their respective days had passed. Still, the phenomenon remains an especially lively example of just how precarious the memories of America and Americans can be. Those who cannot remember the past are doomed to relive it, the saying goes. But it's hard to imagine this particular circus ever coming through town again.

PRODUCED BY LEWIS MILESTONE AND JORIS IVENS

VOICE BY
WALTER HUSTON

Part of the fallout from Hitler's preemptive strike against the Soviet Union in 1941—Operation Barbarossa—was a groundswell of support in the US for these courageous, outmanned, persecuted people. (If there is one thing Americans can respond to, it's an underdog.) Officially, this translated into policy like the billion-dollar Lend-Lease act. But Hollywood also was encouraged—unofficially, it would seem—to do its part in marshaling support for our new ally across the Volga. In 1942, before home-grown projects had had time to be developed, a number of Soviet productions were imported and gussied up for American audiences. Among them were "Our Russian Front" ("See the heroism of men and women fighting on our side!"), with the great Walter Huston providing narration over inspirational stock footage, and "The Battle of Russia" ("One of the Great Motion Pictures of Our Time"—William Shirer), released through the Office of War Information and distributed by Twentieth Century-Fox for the War Activities Committee of the Motion Picture Industry. While not widely seen compared to Hollywood's mainstream product, films such as these (even more of which existed in Great Britain) helped pave the way for the glossy productions that were just around the bend—"Song of Russia," "The North Star," and most especially "Mission to Moscow."

One of the first nondocumentary movies to show our Russian ally's heroic, undermanned struggle against the invading Nazi hordes was this 1943 programmer from Columbia, a studio renowned for its low-budget entertainment. The no-name cast was headlined by young Scotty Beckett, who plays the part of an English lad wandering the Russian countryside in search of the German officer who shot and killed his father. Before his quest is concluded, Scotty helps a ragtag band of Soviet youths defend their village from a full-blown attack. They capture the pride of the Third Reich, and vengeance is Scotty's—although the film ends on a somber note. Propaganda the way it oughta be—short and snappy—although studio boss Harry Cohn would have reason to regret this kind of goodwill gesture when he was called to testify before HUAC a few years later.

A "B" production from United Artists in 1943, "Three Russian Girls" tells the inspiring tale of Soviet volunteer nurses who heroically risk life and limb to minister to the wounded at the front. When Natasha finds an American flyer who has been injured test-flying a Soviet plane (hail, the Allied spirit!), she does her duty. But naturally, the twain fall in love, and when it is time for him to return to the States, she tearfully tells him that she cannot leave Mother Russia so long as there is work to be done. Perhaps they will meet again, after the war? Sure—if the two of them want to be arrested for consorting with the enemy!

REAL ACTION...FILMED
AS IT WAS FOUGHT...
UNDER FIRE!

"
R-F Productions Present

Three
Russian
Girls"

starring
ANNA STEN · KENT SMITH
with Mimi Forsaythe · Alexander Granach
Cathy Frye · Paul Guilfoyle · Kane Richmond

Any kiss may be the
last for these girls in
uniform who live and
love and fight side by
side with their men!

Adaptation by Maurice Clark and Victor Trivas · Based upon photoplay
"The Girl From Leningrad" · Screen play by Aben Kandel and Dan James
A GREGOR RABINOVITCH Production · Associate Producer EUGENE FRENKE
Directed by Fedor Ozep and Henry Kesler · Released thru United Artists

From 1936 to 1938, Joseph E. Davies was the US Ambassador to the USSR He witnessed the Moscow Purge Trials; he broke bread with Stalin; then he cashed in by writing a memoir of his experience. *Mission to Moscow* was published in 1941. A year later the brothers Warner snapped it up and turned it into one of their most prestigious productions. Warner's star team included director Michael Curtiz and screenwriter Howard Koch, both fresh from the enormously successful "Casablanca." Warner Brothers advertised the movie as "So Big . . . So Exciting . . . So American . . . that you must see it!" But at one juncture in the film, Davies says to Stalin, "I believe, Sir, that history will record you as a great benefactor to mankind." Politically correct for 1943, perhaps, but the sort of sentiment that landed Jack Warner in front of HUAC in 1947, squirming as he tried to explain what he had in mind by disseminating such seditious trash. His defense: FDR had asked him in closed quarters to make the film for the good of the American public. True? With FDR dead, only Jack Warner knew for sure. HUAC let him off the hook, but barbecued Howard Koch.

A
WARNER
BROS.
Picture

MISSION TO MOSCOW

Presented in the faux-documentary style of Hollywood filmmaking that came into fashion after the war, "The Iron Curtain" was "based on the personal story of Igor Gouzenko, former Code Clerk, USSR Embassy in Ottawa, Canada." Today that name might provoke little more than a muttered Who?, but in 1945 Gouzenko was in coast-to-coast headlines across the US and Canada for his role in smuggling 109 documents from the Soviet Embassy to the Canadian authorities. The documents proved that the Russians had been stealing atomic secrets from the Allies, and based on them eleven Soviet agents were convicted of espionage, including respected scientist Alan Nunn May and member of Parliament Fred Rose. Gouzenko's reward seems to have been this rather turgid movie about his deed, which is dramatized by actor Dana Andrews as having all the nerve-wracking suspense of a trip to the Bureau of Motor Vehicles. Alas, "The Iron Curtain," for all its topicality, was one of the biggest cinematic bores of 1948.

Run by an obsessive Howard Hughes, the RKO Radio studio was nonetheless as adept as any film factory of the late forties at turning out trim, taut melodramas. In fact, it was better than most. So it should come as no surprise that "I Married a Communist," despite its silly (if accurate) title and overheated dynamics, was an effective yarn. The great Robert Ryan is almost credible as a labor foreman whose youthful flirtation with the Party lands him squarely in its hooks as it plots to take over the shipping industry docks, and Janis Carter is a treat as the "nameless, shameless" woman who seduces his wife's brother, ideologically and otherwise. But the film bombed in its initial release in 1949—limited to three cities—and was withdrawn for a marketing overhaul. It reappeared early in 1950 as "The Woman on Pier 13" with nary a frame cut or altered, but even the absence of "Communist" in the title failed to lure the crowds. Too bad, because this study on the methodology of infiltration is truly the best of its kind.

NAMELESS, SHAMELESS WOMAN!

TRAINED IN AN ART AS OLD AS TIME! She served a mob of terror
and violence whose one mission is to destroy! Trading her love...
yielding kisses that invite disaster, destroy... then — KILL!

RKO
PRESENTS

I MARRIED a Communist

starring
LARAINE DAY · ROBERT RYAN · JOHN AGAR
with THOMAS GOMEZ · JANIS CARTER
Executive Producer SID ROGELL
Produced by JACK J. GROSS · Directed by ROBERT STEVENSON
Screen Play by CHARLES GRAYSON and ROBERT HARDY ANDREWS

RKO
RADIO

If "The Iron Curtain" was too stolid for its own good, this 1949 "B" production was fueled by enough hysteria to send a rocket to the moon and back again. Herbert J. Yates, the president of Republic Pictures, was a fervid anti-Communist, and in "The Red Menace" he made a film that the most intransigent HUAC inquisitor could hug to his bosom at night. Narrated in stentorian tones, "The Red Menace" posits a universe in which every dame is an instrument of the Party, every disaffected ex-GI is a dupe just waiting to be converted. Unabashedly funny to a '90s sensibility because of its overripe dialogue and inept acting, the film does offer a couple of decent jolts. On balance, though, this is the sort of propaganda that only a Joseph McCarthy could ingest without dissolving into a paroxysm of laughter—or tears. The Communist paper *The Daily People's World* reviewed "The Red Menace" as "stupid but dangerous." They were half right.

The text fragments visible in and around the image:

THE SATURDAY EVENING POST SERIAL THAT JOLTED MILLIONS!

WARNER BROS. BRING IT TO THE SCREEN!

ith the soft light of ... ns and the 35,000,000 agraria's activities are crowded

I WAS A COMMUNIST FOR THE F.B.I.

FRANK LOVEJOY

"I was under the toughest orders a guy could get! I stood by and watched my brother slugged . . . I started a riot that ran red with terror . . . I learned every dirty rule in their book—and had to use them—because I was a Communist—but *I Was a Communist for the FBI.*" This was Warner Brothers making amends—in spades—for their 1943 valentine to the USSR, "Mission to Moscow." Jack Warner's *toches* was still smarting from HUAC's hot-seat for that one, so he took no chances soft-pedaling undercover FBI agent Matt Cvetic's preposterous account of his single-handed destruction of Red agents who had infiltrated Pittsburgh (serialized in *The Saturday Evening Post* in 1949 as "I Posed as a Communist for the FBI"). Nasty, racist, and stupid. This rabid exercise in xenophobia was actually nominated for an Oscar as 1951's best documentary. To this day it has never been reissued on video, or within memory been broadcast on TV.

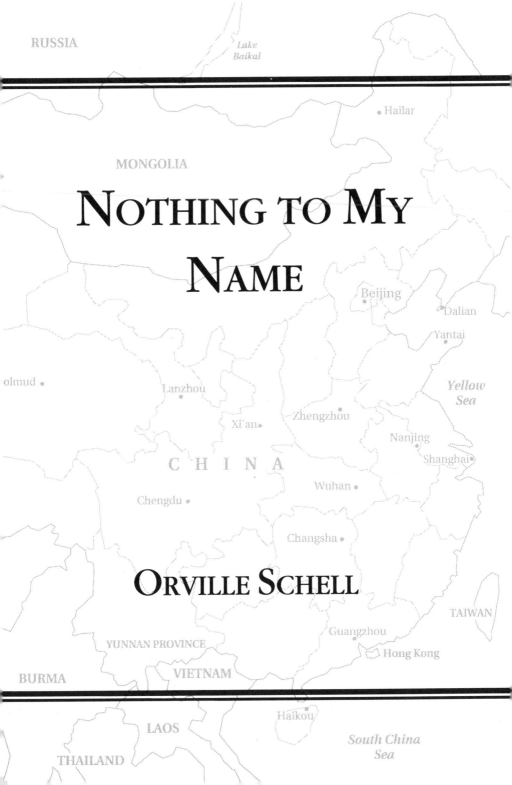

NOTHING TO MY NAME

ORVILLE SCHELL

Orville H. Schell was born in New York City. He received his PhD in Chinese studies from the University of California, Berkeley. He has received numerous awards for his journalistic coverage of China. These include, among others, the Overseas Press Club of America Award for best magazine article on a foreign subject in 1992 for a piece in *The Nation*; an Emmy Award in 1992 and an Alfred I. DuPont–Columbia University Silver Baton Award in 1993 for the report "Made in China" that aired on "60 Minutes" for which he served as program consultant; a Guggenheim Fellowship for profiles of two Chinese dissident intellectuals; and a Mencken Award for an *Atlantic Monthly* article concerning Fang Lizhi. Mr. Schell has been China correspondent for *The New Yorker*, a consultant for "Nightline," and a consultant and commentator for "NBC Nightly News."

Mr. Schell is a member of the Council on Foreign Relations, vice-chairman of Asia Watch, Executive Committee member of Human Rights Watch, and board member of the Yale-China Association. He is a research associate at the University of California, Berkeley.

Mr. Schell, his wife, Liu Baifang, and their sons, Orville, Sebastian, and Alexander, live in California.

In May 1986, twenty-five-year-old Cui Jian was invited to sing at Beijing Worker's Stadium as a guest on China's nationally televised show, "One Hundred Pop Stars," an annual pop-music competition. Until then, Chinese pop musicians had been singing nothing but saccharine love ballads and artless disco tunes copied from the West, so the organizers of the competition and the audience of 20,000 were completely unprepared for what followed. Cui walked on stage wearing a pair of tattered army fatigues. When he began singing in his gravelly voice and performing occasional wild hip gyrations, the audience sat dumbfounded. By the time Cui finished his set, however, the crowd was cheering wildly and dancing in the aisles. In the words of one onlooker, "A new chapter in the history of Chinese popular music had begun."

Cui Jian was born in 1961 in Beijing, the People's Republic of China, one of the most unlikely places in the world to produce a rock-and-roll star. As a youth he was taught music by his father, who played with an Air Force band. After graduating from high school, in 1981 Cui won a position as a classical trumpeter with the prestigious Beijing Philharmonic Orchestra. However, after hearing the music of such singers as John Denver, Andy Williams, and Simon and Garfunkel—whose recordings were among the first nonclassical Western music to find their way into China during the early 1980s—Cui was so taken that he began playing hooky from the Philharmonic, got a guitar, and tried his hand at popular music. In 1985 he formed a band called the Building Blocks with six other classical musicians, thus becoming the first Chinese to embark not only on a career as an independent musician, but as a pioneer in pop music. "I worked hard, said farewell to my old life, and started life from zero," said Cui matter-of-factly about his defection from the Philharmonic.

Living on the fringes of official society was still an extremely tenuous proposition in the mid-1980s. Cui's decision to relinquish his "iron rice bowl"— a Chinese euphemism for the guaranteed salary, housing, and medical care given to all state employees—was an act of considerable boldness. However, while his new status as an outsider didn't promise much immediate security, he was relieved of having to be at the beck-and-call of a *danwei*, or state work unit. This afforded him an unprecedented degree of freedom to develop both his songwriting and his unorthodox life-style. "Of course, when you are the first, there are a lot of problems," he told an interviewer in 1992. "But I also think one is lucky because no one will control you. You can do anything you want."

By 1986, Cui was listening to the Beatles, the Rolling Stones, the Talking Heads, and Sting and had begun playing increasingly more sophisticated pop music himself. But life on the outside was an obstacle course. Even if the Communist Party had not been opposed to "spiritual pollution" from the West, life in a poor country—where access to decent instruments, amplifiers, places to practice, recording facilities, and halls in which to perform was limited—did not make survival easy for an aspiring rock-and-roller. That was when he got the unexpected invitation to perform on "One Hundred Pop Stars."

Cui soon joined forces with several other independent-minded musicians who were kicking around Beijing at the time—including a young guitar player from Hungary and another from Madagascar—and formed a hybrid band called ADO. Playing electric guitars, synthesizers, woodwinds, and brass along with traditional Chinese instruments such as the oboe-like *suona*, the zither-like *zheng*, and the reed pipe *sheng*, ADO developed a unique eclectic sound that mixed jazz, Afro-pop, reggae, and Western rock influences with Oriental flourishes. Band members lived hand-to-mouth, performing on Beijing college campuses; in informal jam sessions at bars, dance halls, and restaurants such as Pierre Cardin's "Maxim's" that ran an after-hours discotheque; and at private parties thrown by foreigners, where they could count on extraterritorial protection from the Public Security Bureau (PSB). Not only was Cui's music ushering nightlife back into Beijing after thirty years of imposed quietude, but in the process he was beginning to gain cult status among Chinese youth.

During the Party's heyday, from 1949 until the late '70s, Chinese leaders had been able to maintain political loyalty by running ceaseless propaganda campaigns. But beginning in the '80s, Western music, films, TV programs, and fashion appeared in China, the result of Deng Xiaoping's new "open door" policy. Faced with such powerful Western pop-culture competition, Party leaders found their powers of persuasion suddenly limited. During these early years of rock music's development in China, hardline Party leaders viewed it as a dangerous vector of both antiauthoritarian attitudes and pernicious bourgeois influences, and they repeatedly attempted to eradicate it. In 1983, for instance, the Party launched a campaign against "spiritual pollution" to rid China of everything from rock music and dancing to makeup and bell-bottom trousers. But because it became obvious to leader Deng Xiaoping that opening the economic door to the West inevitably would bring undesirable "flies and pests" such as Western pop music buzzing into the country, this campaign was soon dropped.

By 1987 it was clear that for many of China's urban young, the mantle of heroism had passed from the likes of Mao Tse-tung to pop-culture icons like Cui Jian and his ragtag band of rock-and-roll nonconformists. Recognizing their dilemma, bolder Party strategists decided that it was time to make a tactical retreat. To make their own political message more persuasive, they began accessorizing it with

117

certain pop affectations. Needless to say, this effort to clothe the Marxist wolf in a Western pop-culture sheepskin created some pretty bizarre cultural collisions.

But if the Party's grand viziers were willing to adopt certain seductive aspects of Western music and culture—even to sponsor disco parties on college campuses and pop-music shows on TV—they far preferred *tongsu yinyue*, or "middle-of-the-road" music, to *yaogun yinyue*, "shaking and rolling music," as rock is known in Chinese. The rock singer Jing Gangshan put the difference between them succinctly when he said, "*Yaogun* musicians sing songs that don't have government approval. *Tongsu* singers sing songs that do." But the differences were far deeper; the very sociology of the two musical forms set them radically apart. The tongsu industry was controlled by the government, which presided over everything from the arts troupes where the songs were written and the singers worked, to the TV shows where the songs were performed and the recording studios where albums were produced. Conversely, *yaogun* was completely controlled by the singers themselves, many of whom were rebels who, disgusted with the banality of *tongsu*, like Cui, had dropped out.

"Rock is essentially a kind of emotional release, something that's out of step with society, a way to let off steam about oppression and depression," rocker Li Lifu told Andrew Jones, whose 1992 monograph "Like a Knife" chronicles the Chinese rock scene. "It's like a public toilet where people can express things they otherwise couldn't express."

The Party, of course, quickly sensed the subversiveness of rock music as an art form. But far from stifling this errant new subculture (which interestingly is translated as *ya wenhua*, or "oppressed culture" in Chinese), the Party's strategy of denying rock bands access to concert halls and excluding them from state radio and television only forced rockers to take root in their own underworld. It was in the privately run bars, restaurants, and dance halls that had begun proliferating by the late 1980s that rock music not only survived, but acquired a new outlaw cachet. This only made it more appealing to the numerous young Chinese who were searching for an alternative to the mind-numbing quality of official Party-controlled culture.

It was not until the 1989 protest movement—when songs like Cui Jian's classic "Nothing to My Name" and Hou Dejian's "Heirs of the Dragon" became the anthems of student protesters in Tiananmen Square—that Party leaders woke up to the real power of rock music as an outlet for youth's pent-up frustration with the system.

"We loved the kind of very strong individual will that was expressed in 'Nothing to My Name,'" 1989 student protest leader Wu'er Kaixi remembered in 1990. "I feel as if the song's title sums up our lives and our sentiments. Just think about our generation. Have we had anything? We do not have the goals our parents were once striving for, nor do we have the kinds of fantastic ideals our older brothers and sisters once had . . . Apart from our strength, we actually have nothing to our name."

What surprised many Chinese observers was how profoundly rock music influenced young student protesters. Hou Dejian, who helped negotiate the withdrawal from Tiananmen Square (only to be detained by police, forced onto a fishing boat, and shipped back to Taiwan), believed that rock music played such an important political role in the protest movement because it allowed young people to experience a sense of inner liberation in an environment where the Party was all-controlling. It was rock music's ability to "free the self from all kinds of repression" that in Hou's mind made it so "subversive." This was also very much Cui's sentiment. As far as he was concerned, real change could not be brought about in China by shrill condemnations of the Party and overt rebellion alone, but only by a less obvious process of internal liberation in which someone must first "feel real freedom."

This does not mean that Cui never raised the political hackles of the Party. One instance was occasioned when Cui revived the old revolutionary ballad "Nanyiwan" as a rock song. This trail-blazing effort to expropriate old Party culture and recycle it with a boogie beat paved the way for the multitude of updated revolutionary songs that would later flood the market. But in 1987 his reworking of "Nanyiwan" was considered a desecration. To make matters worse, its debut happened to coincide with the campaign launched by orthodox Party leaders against "bourgeois liberalization" and "spiritual pollution." After hearing the song, Wang Zhen, the 80-year-old Long March* General who became China's vice-president after the 1989 crackdown, was reported to have demanded indignantly, "How could a young person in new socialist China claim to have nothing?" Cui was expelled from the Beijing Philharmonic Orchestra, banned from performing at commercial concerts, blacklisted on all future radio and television shows, and even forbidden to record his signature hit.

Although Cui's songs sometimes toyed with Party symbols and themes, his growing popularity stemmed more from his skill in articulating the deeper levels of political frustration, sexual confusion, and social alienation experienced by many of his contemporaries without becoming didactic. For example, in "It's Not That I Don't Understand," Cui sang: "Looking back I can't tell good from bad/ I can't even remember the decades gone by/What once seemed so simple is now unclear/And I suddenly feel the world has no place for me."

Ironically, it was Deng Xiaoping's economic reforms that allowed Cui to find a place outside the system of official

---

*Long March—year-long trek by Mao's Red Army in 1935 to escape the encirclement of Chang Kai-chek's nationalist forces.

"work units." As China's economy became privatized and diversified, new margins of society that were just outside of immediate Party control began to appear and to create areas where artists, entrepreneurs, nonconformists, dropouts, and even criminals could find refuge. For a society that had had no such sanctuaries for more than three decades, the recrudescence of these fringe zones represented an extremely important phenomenon.

As Deng's economic reform movement progressed, state subsidies vanished, and state-run companies, including recording studios, scrambled to find new and lucrative projects to shore up the bottom line. When it became clear that money could be made producing rock albums, there were some surprising takers. For instance, Cui Jian's first major album, "New Long March of Rock," was put out by the state-run China Tourism Audio Visual Publishers. Life became easier for "unemployed" rock musicians. The promise of profits had a way of making managers overlook all but the most flagrant lapses in political orthodoxy.

Rock musicians and a new class of pop-culture impresarios—who favored expensive foreign clothes, owned cars, lived in hotels, and dedicated their lives to hedonism and making money—began forging connections with state-run recording companies. "The force of commercial culture is irresistible, and it is affecting every institution," dissident intellectual Liu Xiaobo told me, while in the United States in 1993 lecturing on pop culture. Sometimes entrepreneurs would forgo the niceties of involving a state-run company and simply bootleg a tape: sell it through networks of *getihu*, or private vendors. As in almost every other aspect of life, the market was beginning to create blurry gray areas of cultural and economic activity that were neither officially sanctioned nor completely illegal. And so, even though state-run radio and television continued to refuse to play Cui's music, his underground reputation was expanding so rapidly by word of mouth that he was able not only to support himself from royalties of albums but also to increase his following.

For Cui, the late 1980s were a high-wire act of survival that mixed defiance with compromise. Although he denied that his music was political in nature, its provocatively rebellious spirit and his nonconformist life-style left him ever teetering on the edge of Party disfavor.

In March 1989, during a period of relative permissiveness, Cui was allowed to give a concert at the Beijing Exhibition Hall before 18,000 fans. Once on stage, he pulled out a piece of blood-red cloth from his grungy army jacket, blindfolded himself, and launched into "A Piece of Red Cloth," an enigmatic and disturbing song that is an exploration of the complicated slave-master relationship between oppressed and oppressors. "That day it was you who took a piece of red cloth/To cover my eyes and cover the sky/You asked me what I saw/I said I saw happiness/This feeling makes me feel so good/It makes me forget I have nowhere to live/You asked me where I want to go/I said I want to take your road."

Not only was the blindfold a not-too-subtle allusion to the way the Party had been blinding Chinese, but it made Cui look as if he were about to be put to death. Coupled with the suggestive vagueness of the lyrics, the chilling sight of Cui standing before the crowd in a crimson blindfold created the kind of striking image that made his performances unforgettable.

By April of that year, Cui's reputation had grown to the point that he was signed to a record contract by EMI Music in Hong Kong and was even invited to participate in the first Asian Popular Music Awards at London's Royal Albert Hall. By the time Cui returned to Beijing in May, the Tiananmen Square protest movement was in full swing, and "Nothing to My Name" had become one of the demonstrators' marching anthems. On the eve of the

Tiananmen Square demonstrations, Cui had told an interviewer who had asked if he saw himself as a political rebel, "We do not rebel. We fight for personal liberation." But in spite of such oft-repeated statements expressing aversion to unabashed political activism, as the dramatic events of May unfolded Cui finally could not resist joining the students. And on May 19, the day before martial law went into effect, he made his pilgrimage to Tiananmen Square, where he sang "Opportunists," a song that he had written in support of the hunger strikers. When a wire-service photo showed Cui performing in his signature blindfold before a huge crowd of students, he instantly became identified with the protest movement.

Like so many other young Chinese after the Beijing Massacre, Cui dropped out of sight. After lying low for several months—an absence that spawned rumors that he had been detained by police—Cui was able to emerge unscathed. The next twelve months were not an easy time, however, for anyone living on the slender margins of official Chinese society. With the Party launching yet another campaign against "bourgeois liberalization," and everyone in Beijing fearfully hunkered down waiting to see what would happen, Cui once again found himself reduced to performing at private parties and restaurants, and more than ever walking the fine line between art and politics.

As repressive as the political atmosphere of summer and fall 1989 was, however, it soon became clear that popular music was not to be affected by the crackdown as much as more overt political activities and the press. It was one of those anomalies of Chinese life that while the Party cracked down on almost every other kind of political and cultural expression, they allowed pop music to play on. Even as the repression continued to close publications and politically active workers, students, and intellectuals were harassed and detained, rock bands managed to eke out marginal existences playing in small inconspicuous dives and in the process seemed to serve both as a pressure relief valve and as a surrogate form of protest. As Andrew Jones put it, "Rock parties, wild lyrics, and slam dancing have replaced megaphones, sit-ins, and rock-throwing as the preferred means of protest carrying on the spirit of Tiananmen."

Only a few months after the Beijing Massacre, Australian diplomat and novelist Nicholas Jose happened to visit a Beijing dance hall near Liubukuo—an intersection on the Avenue of Eternal Peace where the slaughter had been particularly horrendous on the night of June 4— and was flabbergasted by what he found. On stage, a band calling itself 1989 I Love You was belting out "Get Back" and "Let It Bleed" as a capacity crowd of young people danced in a frenzy. And before the band signed off that night, it played a deeply ironicized version of the old Party anthem "Without the Communist Party There Would Be No New China" that was reminiscent of Jimi Hendrix's Woodstock version of "The Star-Spangled Banner." According to Jose, the song was a "weird, cacophonous, 20-minute improvisation that could be interpreted as a musical reenactment of events still imprinted on everyone's mind. It was electrifying. Nothing was said, and nothing needed to be said."

By 1990, China's leaders were increasingly desperate to find ways of reentering respectable global society, and they were looking toward the Asian Games, which were to take place in Beijing that fall, as a showcase opportunity. Knowing how important the event was, and always casting about for some way to perform in public again even if it meant making ingratiating gestures toward the government, Cui agreed to do a series of benefit concerts to help the Games make up their huge budget deficit.

His decision sparked some critics to suggest that Cui had "sold out," but it was perfectly in character for someone who saw himself neither as a dissident nor as a Party follower, but as an artist occupying that narrow gray zone in between. And besides, if Cui the pragmatist was to continue surviving by selling albums, he needed to perform and cultivate his fans, even if getting permission entailed certain accommodations with the powers that be. Behind Cui's decision, it was not hard to sense the pulse beat of the market.

At each of his Asian Games benefit concerts Cui Jian was, in fact, greeted by ecstatic fans who screamed their approval, waved posters of him (and Chairman Mao!), raised their fists in defiant solidarity, and flashed the "V" for victory sign like supporters of the protest movement in Tiananmen Square. With the memory of the Beijing Massacre not yet a year old, the government was understandably concerned by these outpourings of support for a maverick rock-and-roller. But what made them almost apoplectic was his habit of donning the blood-red blindfold he had worn in Tiananmen Square to sing "A Piece of Red Cloth."

Not surprisingly, officials canceled Cui's eight-city tour in midstream, and once again he was back playing at private parties and restaurants catering to foreigners. It was not until the spring of 1992 that the Party gave Cui another chance to perform before large crowds. This time it was a series of benefit concerts in Nanjing for Project Hope, an effort by a Chinese foundation and the Communist Party Youth League to assist rural children whose parents were too poor to send them to school. I attended one of them and was stunned to see firsthand the power that Cui and his music had over the audience.

It was raining, but it seemed as if the entire population of Nanjing were headed toward the Wutaishan Sports Arena anyway that May evening. Along every street that led toward the 30,000-seat arena, groups of police officers patrolled as an endless procession of young Chinese flowed by. Outside the gates, crowds of hopefuls gathered to negotiate with scalpers for black-market tickets that cost as much as $25 each—five times their original price, and more than half the monthly salary of the average Chinese worker. An electric excitement ran through the crowd.

In the arena the din was deafening, and the super-charged air of anxious anticipation was only given an added edge by the presence of hundreds of uniformed police.

Even before Cui took the stage, the fans were waving hand-lettered banners and cheering wildly. When the house lights dimmed, the crowd suddenly hushed. Moments later it almost went berserk when the slender, pale, nearly expressionless Cui appeared in blue jeans and a tank top amid a billowing cloud of theatrical smoke and a blaze of flashing colored lights. Cui proudly surveyed his screaming fans and then declared, "Nanjing is another of my liberated areas!" In response to this allusion to the soviet zones that Chinese Communist guerrilla forces "liber-ated" from the Nationalists during the 1920s and the 1930s, the crowd sent up a collective roar the likes of which I had not heard since I stood in the middle of Tiananmen Square in 1989. And it occurred to me that what these fans yearned for was a recreation of precisely the same island of cultural and political authenticity that the Square had afforded young Chinese three years before.

From the moment Cui released the first ear-splitting chord of "The New Long March of Rock," his euphoric young fans were singing along and dancing in front of their seats. It was as if they had been waiting patiently since that terrible day in June 1989 for this single moment of cathartic release. "I love it here so much because I don't have to behave!" a young man sitting near me cried out ecstatically.

While most of the crowd undulated to the rhythm of Cui's music, a block of people just to one side of the stage sat motionless. Compared to the rest of the whooping, clapping, and gyrating audience, it seemed as if everyone within this zone of lifelessness had been anesthetized.

As it turned out, this block of seats was occupied by Nanjing Government and Party dignitaries attending the benefit in their official capacities. It was hard not to feel a certain sympathy for them, helplessly trapped in a scene that was, no doubt, close to their worst nightmares about the insidious effects of "peaceful evolution" and "bourgeois liberalization."

Only the phalanxes of uniformed police officers appeared more awkwardly self-conscious and out of place. Clinging to their walkie-talkies, they betrayed the expressions of awed helplessness that one might expect among firemen watching an inferno burn out of control. And the more excited the crowd became, the more jittery the police grew. Initially they tried to restrain a few of the more rambunctious youths dancing in the aisles, but it was a hopeless task, something like throwing up a wall of sand to hold back the sea. The police gave up and for the rest of the concert remained awkwardly at attention.

It occurred to me that this might be the first time since Premier Li Peng had been forced to listen to student leaders Wu'er Kaixi and Wang Dan during their televised contretemps in May 1989 that representatives of the government had actually listened to the true voice of their young constituents. How much they understood was another question. But they could not have failed to grasp the rough message of these 30,000 youths deliriously cheering a performer who in his oblique but savage way was suggesting that after forty years of socialism, Chinese still had nothing to show for it. "I've given you my dreams, and given you my freedom/but you always just laugh at me for having nothing!" sang Cui.

The dignitaries remained opaque. Only when Cui broke into his song "The Last Shot," I thought I saw a painful flicker of recognition sweep across their faces. I was certain that like everyone else in the sports arena, they were thinking of what had happened in Beijing on the night of June 4, 1989. The lyrics consist of only two lines: "A wild shot hit my chest/And at that moment everything from my life surged through my heart." They were followed by the song's title chanted over and over like an incantation, as intermittent bursts of machine gun-like sound rolled from the drummer's snare. The song closed with a spine-tingling taps-like trumpet solo. As Cui played, his fans—who seemed to have been waiting for the moment—lit candles and began to sway back and forth. The flickering lights created an eerie and funereal atmosphere that only added to the already somber mood of the song.

Cui had insisted that "The Last Shot" was written about the 1979 Sino-Vietnamese war; but the song was so poignantly evocative of 1989 that when his album "Nothing to My Name" was released in China, the lyrics sheet left blank the space that should have held the song's words.

"I don't talk politics," Cui once told Agence France Presse bluntly. "I engage in culture. Politics is not my work." But it was obvious from Cui's concert that whatever his demurrals, his music did tap a deep vein of suppressed rebelliousness in Chinese youth. Whether Cui was seeking it or not, the effect was the same—to arouse powerful, if inchoate, political feelings among his audience.

By the summer of 1992, the Chinese rock scene had become a more robust independent fixture of Beijing's cultural landscape than ever before, and rock musicians had developed a whole subculture with its own dress code, life-style, and language. With "individualism" as their watchword, Chinese rockers favored ripped blue jeans, black leather, silver studs, combat boots, and spiky hairdos. They prided themselves on their profane language and were often more than a little exhibitionist about their libertine sexual mores.

Cui was a leader in this subculture and often pushed up against the very edge of official propriety, but he was careful not to transgress Party proscriptions too flagrantly. In spite of the way he flirted with rebellion and had actually become the figurehead for a whole new countercultural movement in China he never allowed himself to slip into open rebellion. With uncanny accuracy, Cui seemed able to gauge how far he could push without provoking a massive and dangerous counterreaction. In no small measure, Cui's success in avoiding outright warfare with the party was due to his strict abstention from overt political references. It was one of the peculiarities of the political climate of the late 1980s that as long as an artist or an intellectual did not make explicit political statements or engage in direct political activity, it was usually possible to do some pretty outrageous things and still stay clear of Party overlords. In this sense Cui was more of an innovator than a true rebel. He was, however, an extremely influential innovator, who by appearing to eschew politics was ironically able to have an even more profound, if oblique, political effect.

A milestone of sorts was reached in the history of the Beijing rock counterculture when in 1992 Cui and a group of other rock-and-roll cronies pooled their resources, leased an abandoned movie theater in the Xuanwu District of Beijing, and opened it as an after-hours club where rock bands could jam the night away without having to get special permission. Immediately the Taijin, or Titanium Club, as it was dubbed, became the hub of rock subculture musicians, fans, groupies, fascinated foreign students, *getihu* private entrepreneurs, and assorted riffraff looking for "a scene." The Titanium was an unprepossessing windowless hall on the second floor of a drab socialist building. Its only decorations were photos of sundry rock stars and a bunch of old Mao-era records tacked up on the wall. There was a bar that served beer, bands performed on the stage where the movie screen had once hung, and fans danced on the cement floor from which the seats had been removed.

Night after night such rock groups as the Breathing Band, the Patriots from Nanjing, the Beijing heavy metal band Black Panthers, and He Yong played until late at night in a scene like something out of the US 1960s. He Yong was a hard-core punk rocker whose band, Mayday, had been renowned for such songs as "Beijing Punk" and "Garbage Dump," a bleak existential howl of song half-growled and half-sung with a cacophonous guitar line and an eccentric alternating rhythm. Mayday helped put Cui in perspective. Compared to the likes of He and his totally nihilistic musical messages, the cultural iconoclasm of Cui's music was a mere bagatelle. One naysayer, Qu Wei from the Shanghai Philharmonic, railed against Chinese rock and roll and the *liumang* or "hooligan" culture it was accused of spawning in a May 1990 issue of *Wenybao*: "The bourgeoisie of the West use popsongs to propagate their view of life and value system. We should never underestimate [the danger] of this. Our foreign enemies have not forgotten for an instant that music can change the way people think."

While visiting Beijing in the spring of 1992, I stumbled upon a major "gray culture" beachhead where rock-and-roll youth culture and its glorification of *liumang*-ism came together in a way that made comrade Qu's diatribe seem somewhat less delusional. The occasion was a shoot for a film called "Beijing Bastards" that depicted the free-wheeling existence of five unemployed artistic drifters who had dropped out of official life and were surviving by their wits. The film was being directed by Zhang Yuan, a young moviemaker who had made several experimental films and done music videos for Cui Jian. It was being produced with private investment from Hong Kong, along with a new infusion of money from Taiwan.

The subject of the film was none other than Cui Jian himself and the underground rock scene that had grown up around him in Beijing. In a quest for authenticity in this docudrama, instead of hiring professional actors and actresses, Zhang Yuan had chosen to cast rock musicians, including Cui playing himself, for all roles. In fact, the Titanium club had been rented as a set where Zhang could create the proper underground ambiance by shooting bands as they played before live audiences. On this particular night, however, Zhang was doing an after-hours shoot that was supposed to capture the atmosphere of an all-night outdoor rock party featuring bonfires, roast meat, beer, live music, dancing, and even—it was rumored— young maidens who would strip off their clothing in reckless abandon as they danced in front of the camera.

It was just after dark when our rented bus crammed with musicians and hangers-on rattled to a stop in front of a large walled enclosure on the outskirts of Beijing. Upon asking around, I learned that we were at a horse track owned by a bizarre pair of nouveaux investors: Lan Shu, the lead singer of the Black Panthers, and a nameless Russian naturalized as a Chinese citizen who had gone into business shipping burned-out racehorses up from Hong Kong for the riding pleasure of Beijing's equestrian set. Although the film had nothing to do with riding, the walled track provided a perfect setting for all the "Beijing Bastards" who had gathered for the occasion to light their bonfires, play their noisy music, and film their all-night bacchanal.

By the time I arrived, two bonfires were already burning in the middle of the riding ring. Several freshly killed goats were hanging indecorously from a hitching post by the entrance. Near the fires, knots of young men attired in high black boots, tight trousers, black T-shirts, and leather

131

jackets, and a large number of unusually attractive young women in modish outfits milled around in the flickering light, chatting, laughing, smoking, and drinking beer. Since the film crew was just beginning to set up the cameras, I grabbed a can of Qingdao myself and began to mingle. What immediately impressed me about this group of Chinese youths was that they seemed so different from the earnest, righteous, and politically didactic students that had filled Tiananmen Square three years before. Wondering what had happened to "Chinese youth" since then, I asked several members of Beijing's new demimonde if they had been in the Square in 1989. All smiled, said that they were there, and then—as if they had been asked about some relative who had passed away under questionable circumstances—changed the subject. No one seemed interested either in talking about its legacy or politically conceptualizing what was about to happen there on what was, after all, a movie set. What they seemed to want was just to "do their own thing." It was a scene more reminiscent of an American countercultural be-in during the 1960s than anything I had ever experienced (or even imagined, for that matter) in China.

A short while later Cui Jian sat down by one of the fires among a throng of his *gemer*, or buddies, and began vamping on an acoustic guitar. No one seemed to be in charge, which made the scene feel far more like an informal feast than a film shoot. It was not until after the goat carcasses had been unceremoniously hacked into pieces and thrown into the cauldron by two shirtless young men that someone finally rushed out with a clap-stick to start the filming. But by then the party had taken on a life of its own, and amid the prevailing atmosphere of relaxed camaraderie and informality the presence of the rolling camera seemed almost irrelevant.

When I unexpectedly found myself standing next to Zhang Yuan for a moment, I could not resist asking him how the producers of "Beijing Bastards" had secured approval from the Chinese Government for such an unorthodox film. Smiling conspiratorially, Zhang said, "Well, we sort of got it." He winked.

A young woman standing with Zhang smiled and added, "The government says that it wants to encourage individual entrepreneurs as part of Deng's economic reform movement. So we're just taking the government at its word by extending the notion of private enterprise to include rock and roll and filmmaking." She gave a little chirrup of delight.

It seemed safe to assume that the Ministry of Radio, Film, and Television—whose job it was to keep strict account of all movies produced in China—would have been reluctant to give their official imprimatur to a film glorifying the Bohemian life-style of this new class of youths who were out to glorify their escape from the Party's embrace. To tell the truth, it was hard to imagine the authorities even allowing a party such as this to take place, much less an entire film about Beijing's countercultural underground. It was a testament to how things were changing that such outrages against hard-line ethics seemed to go unnoticed.

It was well past midnight before Cui's band actually got wired up and began wailing. As bats flew through the showers of sparks that rose from the bonfires and huge moths did kamikaze dives down out of the night sky into the klieg lights, the electronically amplified sound of band boomed out over the dark fields around the racetrack, loud enough to wake even the deafest peasants in the surrounding villages. People started dancing on a patch of packed earth in front of the band. Instead of moving with the studied awkwardness that had characterized most young Chinese when the first Western dance craze hit China seven or eight years before, these youths moved with a practiced grace and a fluid naturalness that had obviously come from plenty of practice. Feeling very much as if it were I rather than China that was trapped in a time warp, I found myself wondering, even worrying, about the police. Wouldn't they hear the noise and come to inquire what was going on here? After all, few things escape the notice of the authorities in China, and in all my years of visiting I had never experienced anything quite as blatantly Maoist as that evening's revelry. However, no one else seemed in the least worried.

Then out of the corner of my eye I became aware of unexpected movement in the shadows near the entrance gate. Turning, I saw that two policemen in PSB uniforms had come in and were standing in the shadows watching the whole spectacle. I found myself tensing up and bracing for a confrontation. Suddenly the scene being enacted around me seemed awfully fragile.

As I watched, however, nothing happened. None of the merrymakers evinced the slightest alarm. The two policemen simply stood off to the side with their hands clasped behind their backs as if they were watching a track meet or some other informal sports event. In fact, one of them had a half smile on his face, as if he found the scene amusing, or at least intriguing.

After about five minutes, two young men who looked as if they were part of the production team sauntered over to the policemen and began talking casually. Moments later, the police miraculously left. Perplexed, I asked a young man standing beside me if he knew what had happened.

"Aw, they're just locals," he replied without concern. "Unless there's some order from above, they won't bother us," he said, pointing skyward with an index finger. "Anyway, I guess they've been taken care of, so it's no big deal." He took another swig from a can of Qingdao and gazed at the mass of dancers gyrating in front of Cui's band. Then, as if reading my thoughts, he laughed dismissively. "Hey don't worry!" he said.

It was hard to know exactly why the Party tolerated such music, much less allowed such incubators of rock-and-roll counterculture as the Titanium or film projects like "Beijing Bastards" to fester unchecked. When I posed this question to another young man, he just shrugged. "Maybe they just can't control everything."

The truth was that by then so many heterodox ideas, weird fads, and errant cultural tendencies were appearing in urban China, and so many of them were being driven irrevocably by the market, it was hard to imagine how the Party could control them without delivering a deadly shock to the economy on which it relied.

The Chinese government seemed to have decided to triage the situation—to allow culture, like the economy, to have its head while they focused their energies on controlling more dangerous political challenges. There was admittedly a fine line between culture and politics, but by 1992 the general rule of thumb seemed to be that unless rock songs, literature, poetry, drama, or art were explicitly political, it was best just to overlook them.

And while Cui Jian was certainly to be feared by the Party and watched as competition, he had one redeeming virtue: He had repeatedly shown himself reliable not to push too far beyond the limits of Party tolerance. He could be counted on to rein up short of committing unpardonable breaches of Party etiquette and even sometimes to cooperate with the Party for such things as benefit concerts. Thus it was far better to treat him with a certain indulgence rather than oppose him and risk driving him into outright rebellion.

Unlike the students in Tiananmen Square who pushed recklessly beyond the brink, Cui knew when to stop, the better to try again some other day. Cui's pas de deux with the Party depended on his being able to judge where the absolute limits were at any given time. Pyrotechnical leaps that might be interpreted as head-on challenges were to be avoided. Subtle and oblique symbols that conveyed a sense of alienation and even opposition were permissible as long as nothing was spelled out. But by using lyrics that were poetically indirect rather than didactically explicit, and by using music that appealed to the intuition of his audiences rather than to their intellects, Cui could still make his points. He had, it seemed, found the perfect vehicle for dissent during this strange interim gray period of Chinese history. Knowing when to duck and when to weave, when to withdraw and when to attack, when to offend and when to ingratiate, was all part of the ballet that kept Cui from either being stripped of his aura of outsider and maverick, or ending up in prison or exile. His forays beyond official Party culture, during this time when young Chinese thirsted for some expression of authentic artistic feeling, had helped carve out an unprecedented preserve of independent culture that was truly pioneering and accounted for his immense appeal.

But at the same time that Cui appeared to be a renegade, in myriad ways he was still invisibly tethered to the Party. Although he might sometimes push right up to the edge, and sometimes even over the edge, it was the Party that set the boundaries of permissible expression. In this sense Cui was a perfect emblem of the ambiguity of the early 1990s, and a personification of the "gray culture."

POLISH GUMSHOES
FIGHTING CRIME
IN A
PERFECT SOCIETY

STANISLAW BARANCZAK

Stanislaw Baranczak was born in Poznan, Poland. He earned his PhD in Polish literature from Adam Mickiewicz University in Poznan, where he was also an assistant professor. In 1977, as a result of his participation in a human rights group, his coediting of the underground literary quarterly *Zapis*, and his persistence in publishing his own books abroad without official permission, he was discharged by the university. He was forbidden to travel abroad, and his books were banned in Poland.

In 1980, Mr. Baranczak was reinstated at the university and his work appeared aboveground. In 1981 he emigrated to the United States to accept the position of Alfred Jurzykowski Professor of Polish Language and Literature at Harvard University, his current position.

In addition to numerous books in Polish, including translations of fifteen Shakespeare plays, Mr. Baranczak has written *A Fugitive from Utopia*; *Breathing Under Water and Other East European Essays*; and most recently he edited an anthology, *Polish Poetry of the Last Two Decades of Communist Rule*.

Mr. Baranczak lives in Newtonville, Massachusetts. He and his wife, Anna, have two children.

To the outside observer of Eastern Europe, events of significance in that region most likely include the recent parliamentary election, the latest explosion of ethnic animosity, or the current government's budget policies. From that perspective, the political outcome of the collapse of Communism far outweighs any other consequence. But to someone who, like this writer, was born in Eastern Europe and spent a large chunk of his life there, the return of his country to the fold of democratic nations and free market economies also implies other important changes. And if he happens to be a literary critic, for example, the downfall of Communism can translate into the disappearance of a literary genre.

I have in mind the East European variant of what is known in the West as the mystery novel. In Poland, as in the rest of Eastern Europe, the mystery vanished in 1944. When it reappeared twelve years later, the mystery had been transformed.

Anyone who has read a dozen mysteries by different Western authors realizes that this category puts in one basket startlingly disparate works: the classic detective story or "whodunit"; the thriller; the spy novel. Perhaps the chief characteristic that unifies these diverse books is their shared theme: crime.

One can also find other common threads. The crime solver is, as often as not, someone other than a police detective. He is appealing in certain respects, flawed in others and each has his idiosyncrasies. None is above the law. In like manner, the profile of the criminal varies widely.

When the Communists seized power in Poland in 1944, the familiar mystery, the *powiesc kryminalna* or police novel, was banned. After all, its irremovable core was the theme of crime, and crime was supposed to cease in

Communist society.

In 1956, the Soviet leadership relaxed its iron-fisted policies toward Eastern Europe. This led to a cultural thaw, which brought new leaders into power in Poland and a less primitive way of dealing with the thorny problem of mass entertainment. The new Communist *apparatchiks* embarked on a fresh policy, turning the old Stalinist slogan "He who is not with us is against us" into "He who is not against us is with us." Culture was given relatively free rein as long as it did not interfere with official Communist teachings. Morover, since Western pop culture was making inroads into Poland anyway, the regime decided to domesticate mass culture rather than destroy it. If the young can't live without their rock music—why not give them rock concerts with a huge portrait of Lenin as a backdrop? If the mass readership apparently thirsts for mysteries—why not give them novels about crime written exactly like Mickey Spillane's, but set in Poland and employing Polish militia detectives rather than American cops and private eyes?

This argument might have sounded clever at the outset, but it quickly revealed its absurdity. In fact, after having read four or five specimens of the "militia novel" just about anybody might have offered the following definition of that genre: A novel about crime, imitating, to the point of slavish dependence, the Western model, but at the same time serving, to the point of even more slavish dependence, the propagandistic needs of totalitarian ideology.

No one has ever fully succeeded in providing entertainment with one hand and dishing out propaganda with the other. Such a juggling act would require superhuman skills. This illustrates the dilemma that faced every Communist government in Eastern Europe before 1989. The Western model of mass culture, with all its obvious attraction, seemed the ideal vehicle for propaganda; but as soon as it was loaded with a propagandistic message, its attraction inevitably waned. The concept of "Socialist mass culture" was a walking contradiction.

The Polish government made the Western mystery ideologically palatable by establishing certain conditions that it had to fulfill. The first and most critical factor, which all but assured the failure of the Polish mystery, was the precondition that each novel must evoke a "positive hero," specifically, a militia officer*, a police officer in Communist Poland. This resulted in the nearly total absence of amateur detectives or private investigators in all Poland-based mysteries published after 1956. If such a character did appear, the exception only confirmed the rule, because each of these overzealous but loyal citizens ended up (long before the end of the novel, of course) bringing his discoveries to the nearest militia station. Clearly, none of the familiar crimefighters known from the Western mysteries could be transplanted into the Polish setting: neither the Sherlock Holmes-like figure of an amateur detective, nor the Philip Marlowe-like private eye, nor even the commissar Maigret-like French-style police detective. All of them were replaced with the homely figure of a native militia officer. Not only did this narrow the range of possible protagonists to a predictable character, it also cast law enforcement agencies in a favorable light.

In classic detective stories the police have very little to do with the final victory. The Scotland Yard representative usually arrives at the end, and his part is confined to hearing out some Hercules Poirot or other's detailed explanation of why it was the wicked niece Eudora who put arsenic in Lord Fayerweather's herbal tea, and then to

---

*The Polish Communist Party purposefully recast the term "police" as "militia." The latter, especially when accompanied by its corresponding word "citizens'," was supposed to suggest that law enforcement was in the hands of the people rather than under Party control. The term "police" referred only to law enforcement agents in capitalist nations.

making appropriate use of his pair of handcuffs. When the police force does appear in Western mysteries, it is more often than not shown as inferior to the amateur's or private investigator's brilliance, prone to mistakes and heavy-handedness, even corrupt. At least since the '30s, the mystery in the West has made a considerable effort to get rid of the naive equation "law enforcement = justice" and instead to explore the potential gap between these two notions. The even more naive equation "cop = positive hero" has never been a sacred principle in the Western mystery.

In Communist-controlled Eastern Europe, however, the police force was, by definition, an extension of the ruling power, the Party. The Party was beyond reproach, and the same was true of the militia: Each law enforcer was virtually exempt from public criticism, not to mention immune from prosecution in case of any wrongdoing. So when it came to mysteries, Party ideology required that every militia officer be perfect. It would be a gross error to blame Polish readers for the fact that none of the local heroes depicted ever appealed to them. The heroes of mysteries were singularly uninteresting because they were just too perfect to have any life in them. How can a protagonist devoid of faults or flaws be a full-fledged literary character instead of a colorless allegory? An author was hard-pressed to make a militia officer alluring. The author could either portray him as so dazzlingly impressive that readers would be swept off their feet; or he could appeal to the readers' sympathy by portraying the hero as a Superman in a rumpled business suit, exceptional but still "one of us." In either case, the hero had to serve as an allegory of triumphant Justice.

As a result, the more melancholically long-nosed, balding, and fumbling the militia officer was, the more impressive were his supernatural intuition and psychological insight, which allowed him to thwart the designs of the most perfidious criminals. He was sure to have been a war hero in the early 1940s or a man who pulled himself by the bootstraps out of postwar poverty and carved out a career in the militia. At the same time, those humble beginnings did not bar him from excellent education—he usually held a law degree and was fluent in a couple of foreign languages. The most prominent feature of the militia detective was, however, his fanatical love of his work. He was a workaholic on a mission, someone who had devoted his life to fighting crime. The ideal militia detective was, in fact, devoid of all human passions, and his work was a ceaseless heroic struggle. Even if temporarily baffled, every step of his investigation ultimately brought the desired results. This 100 percent efficiency rate made it rather difficult for the reader to question the militiaman's actions from a legal or moral point of view.

In Polish mysteries, militia detectives were always in the right. Searches without warrants, break-ins, provocations, illegal detentions, and even the use of force against the interrogated suspect were always depicted in such a manner as to justify the detective's behavior. If, for instance, at the crucial point of an investigation the protagonist locked up a suspect in his office safe to squeeze a confession out of him (a scene in Artur Morena's *Time Stops for the Dead*), the reader was not supposed to feel any compassion, even though the wretched criminal nearly suffocated. The way the author shaped the entire chain of events leading to that final showdown left the reader no choice but to conclude that the suspect was guilty beyond any doubt; his crime was exceptionally horrible; his confession was the only way to put him behind bars; and he was so hardened a criminal that nothing short of brute force would make him confess.

As a rare exception, a single detective engaged in this sort of private crusade of terror was sometimes portrayed as overzealous, but this did not contradict the general rule either: His mistakes were immediately straightened out and made up for by his superiors and colleagues. The individual was able to err once in a while; the collective, never. In the final analysis, the positive hero of the militia novel was not an individual officer, but the law enforcement apparatus as a whole. In contrast to a Western mystery, it was made clear to the reader that in terms of their sheer number, the technical means at their disposal, and their moral justification, the militia far outweighed their opponents.

But to prevent it from appearing that the militia was facing an easy challenge, the Polish mystery in turn magnified the enemy's power. A single criminal could be promoted to the rank of Great Opponent, a villain who acts on his own but who has almost supernatural powers. An even more frequent solution was to identify the criminal with a larger group—the more abominable and menacing, the better. A gang of drug dealers, an international smuggling ring or, best of all, a foreign intelligence organization were the most popular choices. Not always did the reader realize that, say, a murder that appeared to be the unintended result of a robbery was in fact the product of a "wet job" done by a spy carrying out orders from Bonn or Washington, DC: It only turned out to be so after a lengthy and laborious investigation. Such cases illustrate how the introduction of the theme of espionage was sometimes unavoidable to restore a mystery's inner equilibrium. Only an enemy such as the entire West German intelligence service or the CIA was formidable enough to serve as a worthy opponent to the militia apparatus. In one mystery the protagonist warned his fellow militiaman:

"All this is complicated. Don't forget that we are dealing with a foreign intelligence operation. These are people with high professional qualifications, and we mustn't underestimate them."

However, the awe with which this warning was pronounced was not meant to imply that the enemy was going to win the upcoming battle. Quite the contrary, in the final scene our triumphant hero's comments came perilously close to gloating:

> Major Tomorowski, satisfied with the skillfully accomplished arrest, was in an excellent mood:
> "So this is supposed to be the famous Gehlen Organization? Gentlemen, I blush for you, really." (Jerzy Edigey, *The Yellow Envelope*)

Even the most perfidious, powerful, and relentless opponents were forced to yield, since the militia apparatus was not only their equal in strength and skill but also had the moral right on its side.

The enemy, meanwhile, never exhibited any human trait. Just as the good guy was presented in a manner that left no doubt as to the purity of his noble soul, the bad guy was always shown as an absolute villain. Even if, for the time being, he was a mere suspect, no principle of presumed innocence prevented the narrator from depicting him in such a way as to force the reader to find him guilty from the very start:

> Marcin Pakosz looked scared. His eyes were restless and his palms were sweaty; he dried them time and again on his rumpled slacks, as if he were disgusted with his own hands. (Morena, *Time Stops for the Dead*)

The odious looks and behavior of the criminal found their match in his abominable past. He may have been a wartime collaborator with the Nazis, and from the lowest stratum of society or, on the contrary, the remnants of aristocracy. Even his name may have implicated him. Encouraged by the official stamp of approval that xenophobia received in Poland in the late '60s and the '70s, many authors made a

145

habit choosing conspicuously non-Polish-sounding names for their murderers, sadists, and spies.

In Polish mysteries, the criminal necessarily appeared as odious and contemptible to provide a dark backdrop against which the virtues of the militiamen shone more gloriously. In an Agatha Christie novel, by contrast, it is usually one of the most respected members of a community who turns out to be a vicious murderer; in a Raymond Chandler thriller the surprise lies in the fact that a one-time vicious murderer could have gotten away with his crime and become one of the most respected members of a community. All mutual differences aside, these two classic genres, the serene "whodunit" and the grim thriller, deserve, each in its own fashion, to be classified as *mysteries*.

There was no mystery on the other hand, in a Polish mystery. Nothing unexpected happened. Restless eyes and sweating hands, those symptoms of guilty conscience, never failed to identify the perpetrator. The white-toothed smile and well-tailored suit of the handsome militia officer never served as a cover for corruption or abuse of authority. The roles were handed out and the world never left its designated tracks.

In the end, everything—including the solution of whatever attempted to pass for the criminal puzzle—was predetermined by the ideology of a totalitarian political system with its crude division of the world between "those who are with us" and "those who are against us," its assumption that those in power can never be wrong, its deeply ingrained contempt of anything individual, unpredictable, mysterious, free. The centrally planned economy in Communist countries was not introduced because it promised to be more efficient than the free market system but, rather, because it gave people less freedom. Similarly, the East European mystery novel did not emerge under Communist rule because it was inherently more compelling than the Western mystery but because it was meant to accustom the masses to a vision of the world in which nothing depended on the individual and everything was in the hands of some powerful authority.

Such mysteries are no longer written or published in East European countries. No one prohibited them and, in fact, no one had to: Devoid of official support, they died the natural death of the unwanted, or to put it more precisely, those who have nothing to offer. May they rest in peace.

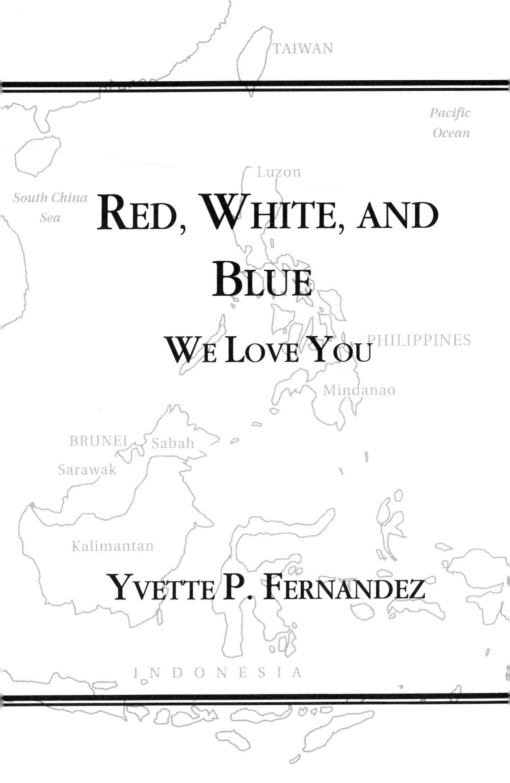

RED, WHITE, AND BLUE

WE LOVE YOU

YVETTE P. FERNANDEZ

Yvette P. Fernandez was born in Toledo, Ohio, and grew up in Manila, the Philippines. She received a bachelor's degree from the University of the Philippines and a master's degree from the Columbia University School of Journalism.

Ms. Fernandez was a reporter and subsequently an editor at the *Manila Times*. Her work has appeared in *New York Newsday*, the *Los Angeles Times*, the *Philippine Star*, and the *Manila Standard*. Her undergraduate thesis was published as a chapter in *Communication, Values and Society*.

Ms. Fernandez is a reporter at the *New York Post*. She lives in New York City.

The unrelenting sun beats down on the people queued in front of the large stone embassy. The American flag waves proudly above them all.

Red, white, and blue
Stars over you.
Mama says,
Papa says,
"I love you."

Filipinos used to be taught that rhyme when they were but toddlers. America, America. The land of red, white, and blue, and oh yes, of American green dollars too. I love you.

Every night, on color television screens in smoky Manila beer gardens, Filipino men watch advertisements of blond, blue-eyed men and women racing about in fast cars, smoking filter-tipped Hope cigarettes, glossy lips revealing perfect teeth, white skin glowing and radiant. America does not have Hope cigarettes, but these men don't know that. They see Americans smoking Hopes on their television sets, so they smoke Hopes as well.

After a hectic day at work, sweating in the heat of a summer night, my countrymen remove their ties and unbutton the long-sleeved white shirts that they have seen Americans wear in the movies. They guzzle San Miguel beer and enthusiastically applaud the crooners who come on stage to entertain them with the latest Madonna and Tina Turner songs. One day, they tell themselves, they will see the real Madonna on stage in America.

Housewives watch Elvis Presley movies and reruns of "The Young and the Restless" on television, too, as they balance crying children on their hips and go about their daily chores: polishing floors with *bunot*, dried coconut husks; squatting on the ground to do the laundry, knuckles raw from the harsh detergent; and cooking their husbands' *kare-kare*—oxtails, tripe, and limp string beans stewed in orangey peanut sauce, or *sinigang na bangus*—chopped-up fish heads, stomachs, and tails boiled with mashed green vegetables: dinners that require hours of preparation. These housewives, too, dream of going to America, the land of floor polishers and washing machines, of Shake 'n Bake chicken and frozen dinners that anyone can pop into a microwave.

In America, they know, they can own their own homes, drive their own cars, select anything they want to eat from the supermarket shelves, and still send left-over American dollars back to the Philippines. With the conversion rate about 25 pesos to the dollar, anyone can easily be a peso millionaire. In the Philippines, only the rich drive their own cars, the rest of the population using public transportation. Most employees live month-to-month, their paychecks barely covering their families' needs. America is the land of dreams.

Every day, hopeful men and women stand in line at the building that can grant them entry into the promised land: the Embassy of the United States of America. They have taken a day off from work, called in sick, made some excuse or other. The children are with the neighbors, a favor that will be returned sometime in the future. The neighbor knows that once the children's mother goes to America, the favor will not be forgotten. *Utang na loob*, it is called, a trait inherent in the Filipino, somewhat like gratitude or appreciation. For Christmas, the neighbor will receive packages of Nestlé Crunch and Dove soap, Revlon Flex shampoo and Jean Nate cologne, Fruit of the Loom T-shirts with pictures of the Empire State Building and the Statue of Liberty. Ah, America the beautiful . . . they have heard the song many times. What anyone would give to go to America!

Outside the Embassy, young paper boys in tattered T-shirts and worn-out rubber thong slippers dart in and out of the winding lines, pushing their fast-selling tabloids filled with lurid stories of sex and violence interspersed with lewd pictures of naked women and dead bodies. Cars and buses with worn-out mufflers and noisy horns inch their way through the traffic on Roxas Boulevard. The stench of dried urine mingles with the aroma of *mais*, boiled corn on the cob, and *turon*, fried sugar-coated bananas piled in plastic basins and hawked by brown women with large arms. Many have brought their own *baon*, but the hawkers are here to satisfy the hunger pangs of those who did not anticipate the long, dull wait. After all, there is nothing Filipinos love more than eating.

The Embassy looms over the lines of my countrymen. At the glass doors stand security guards in crisp blue uniforms, arrogantly allowing their fellow Filipinos to trickle into the building. These guards are employed by the United States government, and they strut about with an air of superiority. They snap rudely at people who step out of line, and smile smugly when they see the men and women react in fear. They act as if they are on a higher plane than their fellow citizens, who arrived here before dawn to apply for a visa allowing entry to the land of their employers. Not that the guards have actually been to America, but the Embassy is considered part of American soil. The guards eat Baskin & Robbins ice cream in the cafeteria, and they use "Made in the USA" notepads and pens in the offices too. The Embassy itself is full of American personnel. They have made a good deal, accepting foreign assignments in this Third World country with its terrible six- to eight-hour-long daily brownouts, its struggling government, its criminal element lurking in the darkened city streets where streetlights have been stolen and the lampposts vandalized, its unending rural insurrections occurring in places that do not even have electricity, let alone streetlights. These American expatriates are amply rewarded for their sacrifice with large salaries, chauffeured limousines, mansions in exclusive subdivisions, and battalions of household helpers to cater to their every need. Their children are schooled in private institutions, with tuition fees paid by the American government as well. It is a good life. During the summer, when the temperature rises and it is too hot to bear in Manila, American families fly home for a vacation to recharge themselves. It will keep them going till Christmastime, when they will once again be able to return to America. Ah, America! The doors open, and the people in line crane their necks to watch as earlier candidates emerge from the antiseptic halls of the Embassy. Some hide tear-stained faces embarrassedly in lace handkerchiefs. Some are venom-spewing, "bullshet you! gahdemet!" They are brusquely escorted off the premises.

I grew up in the Philippines loving everything American. My friends and I played with Fisher Price, Tinkertoy, and PlayDoh and later on, Barbie, Ken, Francie, and PJ. We craved the Chips Ahoy, Butterfingers, and Campbell's cream of mushroom soup that we could buy in the PX stores off Clark Air Base in Pampanga.

Somehow, American servicemen had managed to sneak these goods out to waiting merchants, who could get away with pricing the items exorbitantly. We wandered from store to store, picking up a box of Dingdongs here, some Fig Newtons there. We bought canisters and canisters of Pringle's potato chips and Planter's Cheez Curls, cartons of Bisquick buttermilk mix, and Kellogg's cornflakes. The chips cost about ten pesos a canister; the Dingdongs, twenty-five pesos a box. Considering that the minimum wage was fifty-five pesos a day—the exchange rate was eleven pesos to the dollar—PX goods were only for the fortunate few.

My other source of prized American goods was my maiden aunt, who taught dance in Wisconsin, and who came to visit us every summer. *Tita* Merce was the dream aunt who made me the envy of all my classmates. From her overstuffed suitcases, she would pull out my Aladdin lunchboxes, boxes of Hallmark stationery, sheets of which I eagerly traded with friends, and Danskin tights and leotards that I proudly wore in ballet class. The other girls had to be content with local Yvonne outfits. Oh America, America, what a lucky girl I was.

I loved American books too. My reading went from Nancy Drew in grade school to Sidney Sheldon in high school.

As a result of my exposure to, and my passion for reading, books in English, my grades in Pilipino were the lowest of all. My classmates laughed at my Pilipino and called it crooked, *baluktot*. Luckily for me, thanks to our American-structured education, English was the medium of instruction, with Pilipino being merely a language subject like Spanish or French in American schools. While my Pilipino suffered, my English grades soared. I was most comfortable reading, writing, and speaking in English. To this day I regret not having forced myself to become proficient in my native language. To think that most of our people communicate best in a foreign tongue! Sometimes I think my father regretted not raising us in the national language. While he tried speaking it to us at home when we were a little older, it was too late, and I think he was quite disappointed.

Papa loves everything Filipino. He loves *kare-kare* and proudly declares that his all-time favorite dish is steamed *lapu-lapu* with garlic. I was embarrassed when he wrote that down as his "favorite food" in an autograph book that I had my second-grade friends sign.

For many years, I wrinkled my nose in disdain at many Filipino dishes. While we ate Filipino food in our homes, my friends and I would never think of going out to a Filipino restaurant. In those days we smugly believed that only the *hoi polloi* went to Filipino restaurants. We ourselves went to Italian cafes, Japanese restaurants, and American fast-food joints. Pasta was the "in" thing, as were quiche and sushi. Deep-dish pizza eaten with knife and fork off a plate, and flame-broiled chicken with tortillas were the rage. "America's favorite!" they were touted. "Best in the West!" Anything American was great, and Filipinos reveled in the dry burgers and greasy fries churned out by men and women in red and yellow uniforms.

When I was growing up, Filipino food was everyday food. My mother's ancestors came from Pampanga, the province where the best cooks supposedly originated, and my mother, I always believed, was one of the best. Tessie, our housekeeper, prepared various Filipino dishes three times a day. My breakfast favorite was *daing na bangus*, deep-fried boneless milk fish marinated in vinegar; and *sinangag*, garlic-fried rice, which I mixed with scrambled eggs.

Of course, I never told my friends how much I relished home-cooked Filipino meals; if asked, I would say that I couldn't care less, that I ate whatever was on the table. I took pride in the fact that my mother was also an expert at continental cuisine because Filipino food was *baduy*—tacky, disgusting, low-class. Friends took pride in learning to cook international dishes. They would take cooking lessons during the summer, then show off the latest spaghetti sauce or shortcake they had learned to prepare. They would also proudly declare that they did not know how to cook Filipino food.

Dinner was an important part of family life. On Tuesday nights, my mother's father, *Lolo* Sitong, would come for dinner. All of us would grudgingly turn off the television earlier than usual because *Lolo* was an early diner. We would have crab foo yung, sukiyaki, and other easily chewable food because *Lolo* had false teeth. For dessert, we would eat chocolate bars that we had bought at the Duty Free shops, which in later years replaced the PX stores as the source of imported goods. Over dinner, *Lolo* and my father would have fierce arguments about politics and other topics. *Lolo* never stopped chiding Papa for believing that President Marcos was a brilliant man. Like the majority of the people in Manila, *Lolo* thought it was time for a change, never mind that Corazon Aquino was a housewife. Sometimes we would sit at table for hours listening in fascination as *Lolo* reminisced about his days at Harvard, and how he had become one of the most eligible men in the province because of his American education, and then about World War II and how the Japanese had taken everything his family owned.

Now that I am in America, I cannot help but think wistfully of those long dinners at home in Manila. I recall my *daing na bangus* as I munch on my stale bagel in the New York subway on the way to work, and dream of my *adobo* and *kare-kare* atop steaming white rice as my roommates and I eat our pepperoni pizza or Chinese takeout straight from the box and watch "Jeopardy" on TV. But what am I thinking? This is the land of dreams for every single Filipino who lines up for weeks outside that stone structure on Roxas Boulevard.

Roxas Boulevard with its traffic and noise, its prostitutes and ragamuffin little boys.

Roxas Boulevard with its magnificent Manila Bay sunsets and yet-to-be discovered sidewalk artists, its delectable iced *halo-halo* dessert, and so many wonderful memories.

I miss home.

On weekends, when I should be making plans to see "The Fantasticks" in the Village or "Cats" in midtown, which I've been putting off for ever so long, I find myself yearning to do things other than watch an American play. And then my friend, Leah, calls to say she has a videotape of the latest Sharon Cuneta–Richard Gomez bubblegum movie, rented from the Filipino video store on Fourteenth Street, and off I go to her Madison Avenue flat. Never mind that the syrupy sweet Sharon irritates to no end and that in Manila I would have been embarrassed to be seen coming out of a theater showing one of her movies. Never mind that this is another Cinderella story where Sharon is transformed from poor girl to rich celebrity singer in celluloid minutes. Never mind that Cherie Gil plays her usual role as shrew and Eddie Garcia his customary rich-father one. Never mind that the plot is predictable and we can guess exactly what will happen in each scene. Leah and I laugh at the usual dramatic moments when the villainess slaps the heroine's face; hug our throw pillows and swoon when handsome Richard kisses Sharon after spouting his clichéd lines; shriek with laughter at the fight scenes complete with the sounds of fake punches. Boog! OOoofff! Oomph! We munch our cholesterol-filled *chicharon*, fried pork rind, and complain about gaining weight as we open up little bags of Nagaraya cracker nuts that our friend Don's sister Peachy Pie brought from back home.

As much as possible, we try speak our national language whenever Filipinos get together. Never mind that it is *baluktot* and a little bit rusty. My heart is uplifted whenever I converse in the language of my people. It gives me a sense of identity, a feeling of belonging in this fast-paced world of skyscrapers and strangers.

I didn't know how to react when it was announced in 1992 that the American military bases would be leaving the Philippines for good. With them went thousands of jobs that supported the economies of the small towns around the base, jobs that supported families, fed hungry mouths, sent the little children of the barrios to school.

With them, too, went the PX goods and military surplus equipment. Sorely missed by the upper classes would be the television shows on the bases' American network that households all over Manila had tapped via private satellite dishes. The American military network had offered a variety of programming not available on any of the five local channels, and Filipino TV addicts paid huge sums to receive the transmissions. When the bases left, so did the NBA games and the soaps that Filipinos watched at all hours of the day.

During a two-week trip home a year later I drove through the sprawling, laid-back flatlands of the island of Luzon. My friend Bobby was home too, and we drove to Pampanga, two hours out of Manila, past now empty rows and rows of stores that used to be filled with the PX goods of my childhood. With the United States military bases out of the country, Pampanga, the home of Clark Air Force Base, is once again another provincial area.

I remember driving through Angeles City in Pampanga as a child, staring at the dark women with brightly painted faces, long black hair, and tight jeans who strolled the streets with burly white men in khakis. Some men had a pretty woman on each arm. My mother would attempt to turn our faces away when the soldiers kissed the women in the middle of the street. The women looked thrilled to be with the white Joes with the prominent noses, and turned their own flat ones up in the air. The Joes gave them imported Marlboro cigarettes and lots of Hershey bars. The women's heads were probably swimming, too, with the GIs' promises that they would take them back home to America.

America, America.

When I attended the University of the Philippines, I participated in the anti-American mobilizations on campus. "Military bases out! *Ibagsak ang US Imperialismo!* Down with US Imperialism!" the placards read. Radical students slapped anti-US posters on the walls, urging everyone to stay solid with the movement. Boycott McDonald's, Coca-Cola, Procter and Gamble. Buy Filipino!

For several months I was faithful. I replaced my Crest with Hapee toothpaste, Ivory soap with Tender Care, and I drank the Philippine-owned and manufactured Sarsi instead of Coke. Hardest to give up were my favorite Big Macs and Dunkin' Donuts, but I managed. It was the least I could do to help my poor Filipino sisters who were forced by financial necessity to sell their bodies to the foreign men.

We had to get the soldiers out of there, we believed. We had to stop them from exploiting Filipino women, just as we had to stop their big brothers in Washington from exploiting our already ravaged economy. America was killing us slowly, draining our lifeblood with exorbitant interest rates on our loans—loans that we had begged of them for years—forcing us to borrow new money to repay the old, pushing us deeper and deeper into a debt we could never repay. We owed them our souls, maybe more. Get the damn Yankees out of our lives!

We had banged on garbage cans, blown car horns, launched a noise barrage to make ourselves heard. I did not join them, but groups of activists had then marched across Mendiola Bridge to Malacanang Palace where the President lived, to get their message across to him and his technocrats as well. The anti-riot policemen had squelched the students' ardor with large blasts of water, truncheons, and tear gas.

It was now six years later, and the American Joes were on their way out, leaving the Philippines a sovereign nation. I had long wanted them out of my country, and I was thrilled to find out that we had won, that they were leaving, that they were being exorcised from the land of the Filipino people.

Yet here I was on their land. I gloated that they were

finally moving out of the Philippines, even as I viewed the turn of events from my Manhattan apartment. I was in the land of the American servicemen, fulfilling the dream of millions of my countrymen who would have done almost anything to be in my shoes. I was eating Ben and Jerry's ice cream and wearing clothes from Banana Republic, alienated from my brothers across the seas. What was I doing in America? I loved America, I hated America. I did not know what to think.

Now I turn on the TV in the morning and see reruns of "Charlie's Angels" and "Little House on the Prairie," shows I grew up on. I can flip through over a hundred channels of cable and see just about anything I could possibly want to watch, and yet I turn to Channel 65, where a Filipino entrepreneur has bought TV time to air Filipino shows. I eagerly await the taped news telecast from Manila that is but a few hours delayed, so that I can keep up-to-date on events in the Philippines. It is in English, and the anchorpeople wear tailored suits, like the anchors in America, even if it is much hotter in Manila. Next, I watch the weeks-old canned Filipino variety shows, where the guests cavort in glittery costumes, lip-synching the latest Madonna and Tina Turner songs, with acrobatic choreography to match. The hosts then appear onstage and tell the audience how much they will miss the people of Manila when they take the show on the road to tape a few episodes in America.

America, America. The hosts are excited, I can tell. The members of the audience are excited too. Their favorite English-speaking TV hosts will be able to bring America into their living rooms too.

And one day, if and when the Filipinos back home watching this on television save enough money—and if and when they are given visas by the America Embassy consuls, who are stricter now that the bases are closed— then perhaps the dark men in the beer gardens and the women with the babies will be able to visit America too. One day, they will.

America, America. The land of red, white, and blue...and of green dollars too. We love you.

Glossary

acquisitive—eager to acquire wealth
amalgamate—to join together into one; unite; combine
anarchy—the complete absence of government
animosity—strong dislike or hatred; ill will
anomaly—departure from the regular arrangement
bacchanal—a drunken party
bureaucracy—administration managed by set of officials following an inflexible routine
bourgeois—beliefs, attitudes, and practices that are conventionally middle-class
cacophonous—having a harsh, jarring sound
catalyst—stimulus in bringing about a result
catharsis—purifying or relieving of emotional tensions
chimera—an impossible or foolish fantasy
cohesion—tendency to stick together
consecrate—to declare sacred or holy
conspiracy—the act of planning and working together secretly
contemptuous—scornful; disdainful
convivial—sociable; jovial; festive
decadent—characterized by moral decay; self-indulgent
demimonde—group whose activities are ethically questionable
detritus—accumulation of disintegrated material or debris
diatribe—bitter, abusive criticism or denunciation
didactic—morally instructive; moralistic; pedantic
diffuse—to spread out; disperse in every direction
disconcert—to upset the composure of; embarrass; confuse
dissident—not agreeing; dissenting
dubious—causing doubt
effrontery—shamelessness; boldness; impudence
epistemology—study of the sources and limits of knowledge
eschew—to shun; avoid; keep away from
etymology—origin and development of a word
euphoria—feeling of vigor, well-being, high spirits
evangelize—to preach the gospel to; convert to Christianity
evocative—tending to call forth or summon
exuberant—characterized by good health or high spirits
flagrant—outrageously noticeable or evident
flamboyant—showy; ornate

habeas corpus—right to be brought before a court in a reasonable period of time

hedonism—self-indulgent pursuit of pleasure as a way of life

homogenize—to make more uniform

icon—an image venerated as sacred; a symbol

idiosyncrasy—peculiar personal mannerism

inchoate—just begun; not organized

insatiable—constantly wanting more

insurrection—uprising against established authority; revolt

intangible—that which cannot be touched

intrinsic—not dependent on external circumstances

iridescent—having or showing shifting changes in color

juggernaut—any overpowering, destructive force or object

junta—a small group ruling a country

kiosk—pavilion of open construction

lamentable—regrettable; unfortunate

libertine—morally unrestrained

lucrative—profitable

maverick—person who takes an independent stand

melancholy—sad and depressed

melee—confused conflict or mixture

melodrama—performance characterized by exaggerated emotion

misnomer—the wrong name applied to a person, place, or thing

monopoly—exclusive control of a commodity or service

motif—main theme or subject

neocolonialist—the survival or revival of colonialist pursuits

nihilistic—totally rejecting established laws and institutions; believing that there is no meaning or purpose in existence

obdurate—not easily moved to pity or sympathy; hardhearted

oblique—not straightforward; indirect

obscure—unclear; faint or undefined

opaque—not transparent or translucent

ostensible—apparent; clearly evident

overzealous—too enthusiastic

palpable—capable of being touched

paradox—statement that seems contradictory, unbelievable, or absurd but that may be true in fact

paucity—scarcity; insufficiency
perfidious—treacherous
pernicious—causing great injury; fatal; deadly
phalanx—group of individuals united for a common purpose
phantasmagoria—any rapidly changing scene
philanthropy—desire to help mankind as shown by gifts to charitable or humanitarian institutions
poignant—evoking pity or compassion
procreate—to produce or bring into existence
profane—not connected to religious matters; not holy
proliferate—to reproduce in quick succession
propaganda—systematic, widespread promotion of particular ideas to further one's own cause
proscription—prohibition or interdiction
protagonist—the main character in a drama, novel, or story
quintessential—most perfect manifestation of a quality or thing
retribution—punishment for evil done or reward for good done
rhetoric—ability to use language effectively; language that is elaborate but largely empty of clear ideas or sincere emotion
scrupulous—extremely conscientious
spurious—not true or genuine; false, counterfeit
stoic—indifferent to pain or pleasure
sublimate—to have a purifying or refining influence or effect
subversive—seeking to overthrow or destroy
suffrage—the right to vote
surrogate—a substitute
transgress—to overstep; go beyond
undulate—to move in or as in waves
unequivocal—plain, clear; not ambiguous
vanguard—the leading position or persons in a movement
xenophobia—fear or hatred of foreign people or things

Further Reading

Allard, William Albert. *Vanishing Breed: Photographs of the Cowboy and the West*. Boston: Little Brown, 1982. Nonfiction.

Ardagh, John. *France Today*. New York: Penguin Publishers, 1988. Nonfiction: The author discusses the position of women, Club Mediterranée, *nouvelle cuisine*, and the cinema.

Barson, Michael. *Better Dead Than Red*. New York: Hyperion, 1992. Nonfiction: The author takes a satirical look at the years of McCarthyism and Red-baiting.

Belsito, Peter. *Hardcore California: A History of Punk and New Wave*. Berkeley: Last Gasp of San Francisco, 1983. Nonfiction.

Bromer, Charlotte H. *Unwinding Threads: Writing by Women in Africa*. Exeter, NH: Heinemann, 1983. Fiction.

Bushnell, John. *Moscow Grafitti: Language and Subculture*. Boston: Unwin Hyman, 1990. Nonfiction: Documents the rise of popular culture in Moscow.

Ebersole, Lucinda, ed. *Mondo Barbie*. New York: St. Martin's Press, 1993. Nonfiction.

Goodwin, Andrew. *Dancing in The Distraction Factory: Music Television and Popular Culture*. Minneapolis: University of Minnesota Press, 1992. Nonfiction.

Hager, Steven. *Hip Hop: The Illustrated History of Break Dancing, Rap Music, and Grafitti*. New York: St. Martins Press, 1984. Nonfiction.

Henry, Tricia. *Break all the Rules! Punk and Rock, the Making of a Style*. Ann Arbor, MI: UMI Research Press, 1989. Nonfiction.

Hong, Zhu (trans.). *The Chinese Western: Short Fiction From Today's China*. New York: Ballantine Books, 1988. Fiction.

—. *The Serenity of Whiteners: Stories By and About Women in Contemporary China*. New York: Available Press, 1990. Fiction.

Jarvis, Douglas. *Hollywood 1960's*. New York: Gallery Books, 1986. Nonfiction.

Kaplan, E. Ann. *Rocking Around the Clock: Music Television, Post Modernism, and Consumer Culture*. New York: Methuen, 1987. Nonfiction.

Karnow, Stanley. *In Our Image: America's Empire in the Philippines*. New York: Random House, 1989. Nonfiction: A history of US involvement in the Philippines.

Levitt, Helen. *In the Street: Chalk Drawings and Messages, New York City 1938–1948*. Durham, NC: Duke University Press, 1987. .

Liu, Nienling (trans.). *The Rose Colored Dinner: New Works by Contemporary Chinese Women Writers*. Hong Kong: Joint Publishing Company, 1988. Fiction.

Marcus, Greil. *Lipstick Traces: A Secret History of the 20th Century*. Cambridge: Harvard University Press, 1989. Nonfiction.

McDermott, Catherine. *Street Style: British Design in the 80's*. New York: Rizzoli, 1987. Nonfiction.

Pendergrast, Mark. *For God, Country and Coca-Cola: The Unauthorized History of the Great American Soft Drink and the Company that Makes It*. New York: Charles Scribner's Sons, 1993. Nonfiction.

Stern, Jane & Michael. *Jane & Michael Stern's Encyclopedia of Pop Culture*. New York: HarperCollins, 1992. Nonfiction.

—. *Elvis World*. New York: Knopf, 1987. Nonfiction.

—. *Trucker: A Portrait of the Last American Cowboy*. New York: McGraw–Hill, 1976. Nonfiction.

Wintle, Justin (ed.). *Dictionary of Modern Culture*. London: Ark, 1984. Nonfiction: A reference guide to 20th century biographies.

Index

Index